NEUROPSYCHOLOGICAL STUDIES IN EATING DISORDERS: A REVIEW

NEUROPSYCHOLOGICAL STUDIES IN EATING DISORDERS: A REVIEW

LAURA SOUTHGATE
KATE TCHANTURIA
AND
JANET TREASURE

Nova Science Publishers, Inc.
New York

For permission to use material from this book please contact us:
Telephone 631-231-7269; Fax 631-231-8175
Web Site: http://www.novapublishers.com

NOTICE TO THE READER

LIBRARY OF CONGRESS CATALOGING-IN-PUBLICATION DATA

Southgate, Laura.
Neuropsychological studies in eating disorders : a review / Laura Southgate, Kate Tchanturia, and Janet Treasure.
p. ; cm.
Includes bibliographical references and index.
ISBN 978-1-60741-015-7 (softcover)
1. Eating disorders. 2. Clinical neuropsychology. I. Tchanturia, Kate. II. Treasure, Janet. III. Title.
[DNLM: 1. Eating Disorders--psychology--Review. 2. Eating Disorders--etiology--Review. 3. Neurobehavioral Manifestations--Review. 4. Neuropsychology--methods--Review. WM 175 S727n 2009]
RC552.E18S38 2009
616.85'26--dc22 2009002445

Published by Nova Science Publishers, Inc. ✝ New York

CONTENTS

PREFACE[*]

A number of avenues of research indicate that neurobiological abnormalities may be involved in eating disorders. An important component of this may be some form of dysfunction in cognitive processing. The aim of this chapter is to review the results and implications of previous research into neuropsychological function in Eating Disorders (ED), focusing on the diagnoses of Anorexia Nervosa (AN) and Bulimia Nervosa (BN). Published articles on this topic, uncovered in a recent systematic literature search, are summarised here in a table format, allowing the straightforward comparison of materials, methods and results across studies. Whilst providing insight into potential areas of cognitive dysfunction in this clinical group, the neuropsychological data that exists for eating disorders is somewhat unclear. A number of methodological limitations are inherent in this literature; with issues ranging from sample characteristics to study design and the variety of tests employed, thus restricting the conclusions that may be derived. Suggestions as to how these limitations may be overcome and potential directions for future research are discussed accordingly. We advocate the adoption of a hypothesis driven approach to explore neuropsychological processing in Eating Disorders, the utility of which has been confirmed in the ongoing work of our department. Based on clinical observation and personality research, our hypotheses with regards to reduced cognitive flexibility in individuals with AN have consistently been endorsed. Neuropsychological research has both important theoretical and clinical implications, advancing understanding with regards to aetiology and phenotypes of disorder. The

[*] A version of this chapter was also published in Advances in Psychology Research, Volume 51, edited by Alexandra M. Columbus, Nova Science Publishers. It was submitted for appropriate modifications in an effort to encourage wider dissemination of research.

knowledge derived from hypothesis driven neuropsychological studies may be applied practically in research and treatment settings, with the potential to initiate the development of innovative treatment interventions, as has been seen with other psychiatric disorders.

INTRODUCTION: NEUROPSYCHOLOGY AS A TOOL IN UNDERSTANDING PSYCHIATRIC DISORDERS

Neuropsychology is the science in which brain function is explored indirectly by way of the assessment of human behaviour, incorporating information and emotion processing, response selection and execution. Originally developed to investigate the somewhat gross effects of brain lesions or trauma, neuropsychological assessments are increasingly being used and have shown utility in the examination of psychiatric populations where impairments of cognitive functioning are much less severe. Neuropsychological assessment involves conducting a series of structured tests which are thought to be reliable and valid measures of cognitive functioning in an attempt to delineate cognitive deficits and identify putative anatomical areas of dysfunction.

Neuropsychological data can potentially be used to provide novel information and advance our understanding of psychiatric disorders in a number of ways (Keefe, 1995). Data may be used to predict prognosis or course of illness and also assist in the development of treatment strategies, informing about the presence of specific deficits which may benefit from cognitive remediation programmes or identifying strengths which may be built upon and utilised for therapeutic purposes. As well as clinical applications, neuropsychology is increasingly being employed in the research field, contributing to theoretical advances which in turn have important clinical implications. The identification of underlying sub-types of heterogenous disorders based on cognitive processing, is an example of how neuropsychological data could contribute to the refinement of diagnostic classifications, enhancing our understanding of illness phenotypes and aetiological processes. Recent research developments have seen the utilisation of neuropsychological tasks in conjunction with powerful brain imaging technology, to obtain direct measures of brain function and reveal the neurobiological correlates of cognitive dysfunction (Rubia, 2002). The application of neuropsychology as a research tool has produced a vast literature across various psychiatric disorders and several systematic reviews have sought to determine the specific profile of cognitive deficits associated with psychiatric illnesses, such as schizophrenia (Heinrichs & Zakzanis, 1998), bipolar disorder (Quraishi & Frangou, 2002) and obsessive-compulsive disorder (Kuelz, Hohagen, & Voderholzer, 2004).

Whilst the potential for major advances in understanding from neuropsycholgical research is clear, limited gains have been made in the study of EDs, despite growing interest in this field and the obvious links between ED symptomatology and maladaptive cognitive processes. A potential reason for this may be due to the lack of a clear theory or model upon which research studies have been designed. As highlighted in the later sections of this chapter, we advocate the use of a hypothesis driven approach to neuropsychology, specifically based upon our knowledge concerning vulnerability traits in EDs. Investigating whether the presence of such traits has neurobiological relevance, could enable the development of cognitive models upon which future research may be based. We consider neuropsychology to be an essential tool in the exploration of biological phenotypes in EDs, and their potential involvement in the vulnerability and maintenance of disorder as a highly important area for research development.

The study of brain-behaviour relationships is complex, and requires the understanding of biological systems and potential confounding variables. In order to utilise neuropsychology to its full potential in the future, there is a need to review the existing literature relating to neuropsychological processing in EDs so that general conclusions can be derived and necessary advances in methodology may be determined.

Chapter 1

EVIDENCE TO SUGGEST NEUROBIOLOGICAL DYSFUNCTION IN EATING DISORDERS

Several lines of evidence suggest that the EDs are associated with neurobiological anomalies, all of which converge towards the potential for dysfunctional cognitive processing. Whilst an exhaustive review of the literature is not permitted here, the research areas of relevance are briefly highlighted.

BRAIN DEVELOPMENT AND AGE OF ONSET

Pregnancy and birth complications (PBCs) have been associated with anomalous brain structure and impairments in neurotransmitter systems, both of which have been found in some individuals with AN (Bakan, Birmingham, & Goldner, 1990). Gestational age and high numbers of complications in pregnancy are associated with increased risk of AN (Foley, Thacker, Aggen, Neale, & Kendler, 2001), in addition to low birth weight for gestational age and birth trauma (Cnattingius, Hultman, Dahl, & Sparen, 1999). Maternal stress and anxiety during pregnancy is also associated with aberrant brain development (Lou, Hansen, Nordentoft, & Pryds, 1994; O'Connor, Heron, Golding, Beveridge, & Glover, 2002), and again elevated levels of maternal anxiety have been reported in AN samples, (Shoebridge & Gowers, 2000). Therefore, aberrant brain development may be present amongst some individuals with EDs, specifically those with AN.

The greatest period of risk for the development of an eating disorder, adolescence, corresponds with an crucial time for brain development, involving the maturation of the frontal lobes (Gogtay et al., 2004). Whilst the direction of causation between psychiatric illness and anomalous brain development is difficult to establish, any interference in such developmental processes could result in structural and functional anomalies in this brain region known to be critically involved in cognitive processing (especially executive functioning), emotion regulation and personality characteristics (Cummings, 1993).

The consequences of adverse perinatal and neonatal factors on biological and psychosocial development and the changes that occur in these realms during puberty, have been incorporated in a recent neurodevelopmental model for AN (Connan, Campbell, Katzman, Lightman, & Treasure, 2003). Lena, Fiocco and Leyenaaer (2004) have proposed mechanisms through which the putative presence of premorbid cognitive deficits in adolescence may serve as vulnerability factors in the development of EDs. The authors suggest that anomalous cognitive function may have detrimental effects on physical and emotional maturation, interpersonal relationships, sense of autonomy and self-esteem.

Neurotransmitter Function

Neurotransmitters are chemical messengers in the brain which affect how information is processed and therefore how we think and behave. Anomalous levels of certain neurotransmitters have been found in individuals with EDs, during the phase of acute illness and at weight restoration or recovery, thus being implicated as potential trait related dysfunctions which may play a role in the pathogenesis of disorder (Kaye et al., 2001; Kaye, Frank, & McConaha, 1999; Frank et al., 2001). Of particular relevance are the neurotransmitters serotonin and dopamine. Serotonin (5HT) has been traditionally thought to play a role in behavioural inhibition, being involved in the regulation of many biological systems including feeding behaviour and emotion processing, both of which are maladaptive in EDs (Brewerton, 1995). It is also thought to be involved in the regulation of affect, impulse–related disorders and personality characteristics (Lucki, 1998) high levels being associated with inflexibility and obsessive-compulsive behaviour, low levels with impulsivity and disinhibition (including substance abuse, suicidality, gambling, antisocial behaviour), again features that have been found in both AN (Fessler, 2002) and BN (Newton, Freeman, & Munro, 1993; Steiger, Israel, Gauvin, Kin, & Young, 2003; von Ranson, Kaye, Weltzin, Rao, & Matsunaga, 1999). Dysregulation of dopamine function has been implicated as a potential contributor to anorexia nervosa, specifically the restricting subtype, (Kaye et al., 1999). Dopamine has been associated with neuropsychological functions relating to the regulation of attention and behaviour, motor activity, sensitivity to reward and novelty seeking (Bardo, Donohew, & Harrington, 1996; Cools, Barker, Sahakian, & Robbins, 2003; Cannon & Bseikri, 2004).

NEUROIMAGING

Structural and functional neuroimaging studies have identified the presence of brain dysfunction in eating disorders, providing direct evidence to support the involvement of the frontal lobes in EDs, as implicated by personality and behaviour research (Uher, Treasure, & Campbell, 2002).

Studies investigating brain structure in AN have highlighted anomalies consisting of enlarged ventricular and sulcal volumes during acute illness state (Katzman, Christensen, Young, & Zipursky, 2001), contributing to a decrease in overall grey and white matter (Uher et al., 2002). Whilst these abnormalities have been seen to be reversible with weight gain and thus termed 'pseudoatrophy' (Sein, Pearson, Nicol, & Hall, 1981), there is evidence to suggest that structural change is not completely reversible (Kingston, Szmuckler, Andrews, Tress, & Desmond, 1996; Lambe, Katzman, Mikulis, & Kennedy, 1997). Enlarged ventricles have also been reported in BN (Lauer, Laessle, & Fichter, 1990), thus indicating that atrophy may not just be attributed to emaciation alone.

Perhaps of most relevance to the question of neuropsychological function in EDs is the research that has explored cerebral activity. Both AN and BN groups have shown reduced brain metabolism at rest (Delvenne, Goldman, De, & Lostra, 1999) with anomalous activity in prefrontal areas in response to symptom specific stimulation (Nozoe et al., 1993; Nozoe et al., 1995). Most recently, in the largest fMRI study of this clinical group and the first to directly compare different ED diagnoses, Uher et al., (2004) report abnormal prefrontal reaction to symptom-related (food stimuli) but not to standard emotional images in both AN and BN, involving the orbitofrontal cortex and the anterior cingulate. Additionally, diagnosis specific activations were found in the anterior and lateral prefrontal cortex in response to food stimuli (Uher et al., 2003). Anomalous activation of the prefrontal cortex in response to disease-specific stimuli has also been found in participants with long-term recovery from AN, signifying a potential scar of the illness or trait related neural correlate (Uher et al., 2003). The prefrontal cortex is an area of the brain involved in cognitive processing, crucial for carrying out executive functions such as cognitive flexibility, planning and response inhibition (Robbins, 1996). The presence of functional anomalies in this area thus highlights the potential for underlying problems in information processing in AN and BN.

Chapter 2

LITERATURE REVIEW

GENERAL REVIEW OF THE NEUROPSYCHOLOGICAL LITERATURE RELATING TO EATING DISORDERS

Previous reviews on the topic of neuropsychological function in EDs have been published, however these have not been conducted in a systematic way (Lauer, 2002; Lena, Fiocco, & Leyenaar, 2004). Much of the neuropsychological data available is confusing, with contradictory results and methodological problems limiting the conclusions that may be derived (Tchanturia, Campbell, Morris, & Treasure, in press). Despite this, there appears to be a general consensus that EDs are associated with anomalous information processing, albeit subtle. As highlighted by Lauer (2002), the most consistent reports of cognitive dysfunction relate to attentional deficits, involving selective attention (enhanced distractibility) and flexibility/inhibition functions (response selection). Indeed the largest body of research related to cognitive function in EDs has focused on attentional bias and interference control. Paradigms such as the emotional stroop task have consistently shown that both individuals with AN and BN show information processing biases with specific stimuli related to ED psychopathology. These results are in line with the typical clinical observations regarding preoccupation with food and food related activities and the over-concern with eating, shape and weight issues. Attention and memory biases towards emotional relevant (symptom related) stimuli have been reported to be present during acute and recovered illness states, and as such could be factors involved in treatment resistance, symptom maintenance and relapse risk. This specific body of research will not be discussed here further as two detailed reviews have recently been published on this topic, one a meta-analysis from a systematic review (Dobson & Dozois, 2004) and the other a narrative review, (Lee & Shafran, 2004). The remainder of this chapter will focus on studies investigating the integrity of more general cognitive functions, involving tasks and stimuli which are not specifically related to ED psychopathology.

We have recently undertaken a systematic search of the available literature using the terms neuropsychology, anorexia, bulimia, cognitive performance and executive functions using the electronic databases PsycInfo, Medline and Web of Science. Additional hand searches through reference lists and specialist ED journals identified further articles of relevance. A total of fifty two studies were found and are displayed chronologically in table 2. Whilst acknowledging the problem relating to the impurity of many neuropsychological tests, the following qualitative review of the literature is organised according to the putative cognitive functions measured. Conducting this review has made the contradictory nature of research findings apparent. Possible reasons for divergent results are discussed at length in the later section of this chapter entitled 'methodological considerations'.

Chapter 3

REVIEW OF AN LITERATURE

INTELLIGENCE

Intelligence tests are incorporated into neuropsychological batteries to ensure that the groups under study have equivalent general information processing capabilities. However, the study of IQ has been interesting in itself in the ED literature as individuals, especially with AN have typically been characterised as being high achievers academically, with frequent anecdotes of striving for and attaining the best marks at school. This lead some to speculate that individuals with AN have higher than average IQs. Whilst ED samples have been to found to have higher IQs than other psychiatric groups (Blanz, Detzner, Lay, Rose, & Schmidt, 1997), in general, the evidence suggests that intelligence levels do not exceed general population norms. In overcoming the methodological limitations of small sample sizes and selection bias, Ranseen and Humphries (1992) found that general intellectual functioning across the diagnoses of AN and BN was equivalent to published norms. Using a population based sample of individuals who had previously had AN but had achieved weight restoration, Gillberg, Gillberg, Rastam and Johansson (1996) also indicated that IQ was not inflated in this group and was inline with that of the healthy comparison participants. Dura and Bornstein (1989) attributed the high academic achievement displayed in their limited AN sample to the pervasive personality attribute of 'perfectionistic striving', as achievement scores were found to be greater than the ability levels indicated by IQ testing. The authors highlight that this is in contrast to other psychiatric disorders in which the relationship between IQ and attainment is often in the reverse, with achievements not matching true capability as indicated by assessments of IQ. Therefore the literature suggests that whilst they are not intrinsically more intelligent than the general population, individuals with AN maybe more diligent in their work and expend more effort in order achieve high grades and to be 'perfect' or 'model' students.

ATTENTION

Many reports of neuropsychological deficits in AN have been interpreted as being attentional in nature, however there are many different facets of attention processing, typically divided into the domains of 'vigilance', 'divided attention' and 'speed of information processing'.

In general it appears that basic attention abilities such as attention span and general alertness are relatively preserved in AN. Out of the many studies employing tasks such as the trail-making test (part a), digit span and letter cancellation, few have reported deficits in these areas (Jones, Duncan, Brouwers, & Mirsky, 1991; Szmukler, Andrewes, Kingston, & Chen, 1992). Speed of information processing has shown to be anomalous in AN, with slow reaction times being associated with poor prognosis (Hamsher, Halmi, & Benton, 1981).

Continuous performance tasks are the most popular form of test used to assess vigilance or sustained attention. Consistent reports of poor vigilance skill are found in the studies of Seed et al., (2000; 2002) in line with previous findings (Laessle, Fischer, Fichter, Pirke, & Krieg, 1992). However these contrast with reports of 'normal' vigilance performance by other research groups (Green, Elliman, Wakeling, & Rogers, 1996; Bradley et al., 1997; Jones et al., 1991; Bayless et al., 2002).

In comparison to the uniform results found with the emotional stroop paradigms, the use of the traditional stroop task to investigate divided attention has produced conflicting results. Whilst some studies have not found general problems in selective attention (Ben-Tovim, Walker, Fok, & Yap, 1989; Cooper & Todd, 1997; Perpina, Hemsley, Treasure, & de Silva, 1993) it is apparent in a number of studies that some participants with AN do show non-specific attentional biases, showing deficient performances with stimuli unrelated to their ED concerns (Fassino et al., 2002; Kingston et al., 1996; Ohrmann et al., 2004; Szmukler et al., 1992).

In summary, rather than selective deficits being reported, the literature provides numerous examples of dysfunction in the domains of vigilance (Laessle, Krieg, Fichter, & Pirke, 1989; Seed, Dixon, McCluskey, & Young, 2000; Seed, Mccue, Wesnes, Dahabra, & Young, 2002; Fassino et al., 2002) and divided attention (Kingston et al., 1996; Lauer, Gorzewski, Gerlingloff, Backmund, &

Zihl, 1999). The relatively robust findings of attention deficits indicate increased susceptibility to interference in this clinical group which in turn may contribute to sub-optimal performance in tasks designed to assess other cognitive functions. The importance of intact attention processing is especially apparent in many executive function tasks and is a basic requirement for the encoding of relevant information into storage and its subsequent retrieval in memory tasks. The problem of 'cross contamination' in testing will be considered in the discussion of methodological problems in the current literature. A number of theories have been proposed to try and explain the general attention deficit found in AN. It has been suggested that dysfunctional attention processing could be caused by a "disturbance of arousal mechanisms or disturbance with motivation due to endogenous distractions (preoccupation with other concerns)" (Hamsher et al., 1981, p. 85). More recently Dodin and Nandrino (2003), also referred to the arousal level of participants, proposing that high levels of anxiety result in the preference for controlled information processing which in turn uses up cognitive resources and impedes the appropriate selective processing of relevant information.

MEMORY AND LEARNING

Deficits have been reported amongst AN samples in long-term, short-term or working memory and general learning ability tasks, in both verbal and visual domains (e.g. Murphy et al., 2002; 2004; Seed et al., 2002). As highlighted above, some of these results are thought to be related to problems in attention processing. Seed et al., (2000) found that it was only in the presence of distracting stimuli that memory deficits became apparent, highlighting a role of attention processing in memory skills. In accordance, Dodin and Nandrino, (2003) posit that the inability to filter out irrelevant stimuli (irrespective of the emotional valence of the stimuli) results in working memory saturation and dysfunction. The studies of Murphy et al., (2004; 2002) demonstrated differential deficits of learning ability in AN, with participants displaying poor conditional-associative-learning skills with neutral stimuli in relation to normal performance with individually threatening stimuli, specifically, illness related words. Matching the performance pattern seen in OCD (Murphy, Nutzinger, Paul, & Leplow, 2004), it was proposed that the preserved learning ability seen when the tasks involved threatening stimuli could be attributed to hyperactivity of the 'Behavioural Inhibition System'(Gray & McNaughton, 2000), resulting in increased arousal and attention to such stimuli and thus superior task performance under these specific conditions (Murphy, Nutzinger, Paul, & Leplow, 2002).

Strupp, Weingartner, Kaye and Gwirtsman, (1986) were the first to specifically investigate potential differences in the performance of automatic and effortful information processing tasks amongst AN participants, using tasks of recall and recognition. As hypothesised, whilst showing equivalent (and in one recall test enhanced) performance with controls in the effortful learning tasks, AN participants showed deficits in tests which assessed automatic or incidental processing. The authors explained this performance pattern as being suggestive of hyperarousal in AN, narrowing attentional focus and reducing cognitive capacity such that the task at hand may be performed successfully with limited processing of extraneous aspects. Further evidence of this has been reported more recently by Galderisi et al., (2003) with AN participants again displaying impairment in non-effortful learning tasks whilst showing enhanced effortful processing.

In comparison to those above, there are studies that have highlighted deficits in memory and learning which appear to be independent of attention processes. Problems suggestive of a reduction in working memory capacity have been reported (Green et al., 1996; Kingston et al., 1996; Mathias & Kent, 1998) and Mathias and Kent (1998) found that in the absence of broad neuropsychological deficits, problems in the ability to recall verbal information was most prominent. Further contradictions exist in the literature as some authors report the preservation of general memory processes (Murphy, Smith, Cowen, Robbins, & Sahakian, 2002; Lauer et al., 1999) and learning ability (Mathias and Kent, 1998) in AN, including 'normal' performance being displayed in conditional-associate learning tasks (Seed et al., 2000; Bradley et al., 1997).

Motor Function

It is important to investigate motor speed and reaction times as indicators of psychomotor ability as these are critical variables in the performance of most neuropsychological tasks (Lauer, 2002). Using simple reaction time and motor tasks such as finger tapping, it appears that AN participants show psychomotor slowing (Green et al., 1996; Kingston et al., 1996; Szmukler et al., 1992). These problems have been found to remain following weight gain (Hamsher et al., 1981; Kingston et al., 1996). The Dysdiadochokinesis test is a neurological task which involves specific arm movements (alternating between pronation and supination) in a limited space of time. Performance in this task is impaired both during acute illness and following recovery amongst AN participants (Gillberg, Rastam, &

Gillberg, 1994; Rastam, 1992; Holliday, Tchanturia, Landau, Collier, & Treasure, in press; Tchanturia et al., 2004a).

Using more complex tasks in which motor speed is thought to be an important component (e.g. digit-symbol and trail-making tests), some authors report normal speed and efficiency of motor processing in AN (Murphy et al., 2002; Witt, Ryan, & Hsu, 1985). Furthermore Pieters et al., (2003) reported that contrary to the majority of previous findings, their participants with AN performed with faster reaction times in a drawing copy task. Thus impaired performance across neuropsychological tasks can not just be attributed to reduced efficiency of motor function.

Haptic tasks: Haptic tasks require the integration of complex sensorimotor information, where changes in the receptors of joints, tendons, muscles and skin can provide information about the spatial characteristics of objects being explored in a tactile way (Grunwald, Ettrich, Assmann, Daehne, & Krause, 2001). The studies of Grunwald et al; (2002; 2001), Tchanturia et al., (2001; 2002; 2004; 2004b) and Holliday et al., (in press) all indicate that anomalous haptic processing can be found in AN and that this dysfunction appears to be independent of illness state. Tchanutria et al., (2001; 2002; 2004a; 2004b) and Holliday et al., (in press) found that AN participants were more susceptible to perceptual illusions in tasks requiring the haptic exploration of objects. Linking neuropsychological data with direct measures of brain processing, in this case electroencephalogram (EEG), Grunwald et al., (2001) concluded that AN is associated with dysfunction in the right hemisphere parietal lobe.

VISUO-SPATIAL PROCESSING

Both strengths and weaknesses have been uncovered in this domain. Many studies have reported the presence of deficits in visuo-spatial processing in AN, using tasks such as block design, rey figure (copy), embedded figures and line orientation tasks (Bowers, 1994 Gillberg, 1996; Fox , 1981; Jones et al., 1991; Kingston et al., 1996; Szmuckler et al., 1992). The presence of underlying visuo-spatial deficits have been suggested to contribute to the pervasive problems related to body image/perception in this clinical group and supports the hypothesis regarding a right-hemisphere dysfunction in EDs (Braun & Chouinard, 1992). However the results of Mathias and Kent (1998) and Bradley et al., (1997) did not highlight impairment in visuo-spatial processing, challenging this theory. Furthermore, whilst Gillberg et al., (1996) reported poor performance in object assembly, their AN participants performed as well as controls in another visuo-spatial task, the block design test. Performance in block design has been shown to be aided by a piecemeal processing style, as seen in individuals with autism who display 'weak central coherence', a bias in cognitive style towards local over global information processing, (Happe, 1999). Gillberg et al., (1996) posited that the differential performance seen across tasks was indicative of a specific response style, as opposed to evidence of a visuo-spatial deficit *per se.* It was speculated that the AN participants focus on individual details of task stimuli, rather than processing the gestalt. This cognitive style is advantageous in block design (as highlighted above), where as to perform the object assembly task optimally, details should be disregarded in favour of processing the stimuli as a whole. A preference for piecemeal rather than global information processing in AN may also explain performance deficits in the rey figure copy test (Jones et al., 1991; Kingston et al., 1996) and a version of the Bender Gestalt Test (Bowers, 1994), both requiring the processing of a global design rather than local aspects of stimuli. Thus it appears that cognitive style may account for both optimal and impaired performance across different visuo-spatial tasks, depending on their processing requirements. The preoccupation with detail concords to many clinical features of AN and this information processing style has been indicated in both our clinical and research work conducted at the Institute of Psychiatry, London (Davies & Tchanturia, In press; Holliday, personal communication). Our pilot data indicates that individuals with a history of AN show superior performance in block design, in the presence of impairment on the object assembly test and the copy subtest of the rey figure (Holliday, personal communication). These findings point to a preferential cognitive style in line with the weak central coherence associated with Autism (Happe, 1999). Further work is underway in our department to explore and replicate this intriguing data.

Executive Functions

The term 'executive function' relates to higher-order cognitive processes which "enable a person to engage successfully in independent, purposeful, self serving behaviour" (Lezak, 1995, p.42). Little is known with respect to the exact nature of executive functions, including their organisation and functional role in human cognition (Miyake, Friedman, Emerson, Witzki, & Howerter, 2000). This lack of understanding has contributed to different sub-classifications or fractionation of functions being proposed, however cognitive skills such as fluency, planning, cognitive flexibility, problem solving, response inhibition, decision making and prospective memory are typically thought to be components of this umbrella term (Spreen & Strauss, 1998; Burgess, 1997).

Set shifting: The most consistent executive function deficit found in the AN literature involves set shifting ability or 'switching'. Set shifting is an essential component of cognitive and behavioural flexibility involving the ability to direct attention away from a previously relevant stimulus dimension towards one that was previously irrelevant, thus allowing the adaptation of behaviour in line with changing demands of the environment. This adaptive behaviour has been termed 'reactive flexibility'(Eslinger & Grattan, 1993). Problems in set shifting may manifest itself in a variety of forms related to cognitive inflexibility (e.g. concrete and rigid approaches to problem solving and stimulus bound behaviour) and response inflexibility (e.g. perseverative or stereotyped behaviours). A number of neuropsychological tests have been designed to assess cognitive flexibility, such as the Wisconsin Card Sorting Test (WCST) and the Trail Making Test (TMT). The majority of studies that have investigated set shifting ability have reported reduced flexibility in AN samples (Bowers, 1994; Fassino et al., 2002; Fox, 1981; Jones et al., 1991; Holliday et al., in press; Lauer et al., 1999; Lawrence et al., 2003; Tchanturia et al., 2004a; Tchanturia et al., 2004b; Tchanturia, Morris, Surguladze, & Treasure, 2002; Tchanturia, Serpell, Troop, & Treasure, 2001).

Fluency: Considered to be a separate component of cognitive flexibility, fluency measures are used to assess 'spontaneous flexibility'(Eslinger et al., 1993). This term has been used to refer to the ability to rapidly produce a flow of ideas and answers according to a given constraint, requiring divergent thought and behaviour. Studies that have investigated verbal fluency performance (both letter and category) in AN report that this executive function is preserved (Bayless et al., 2002; Hamsher et al., 1981; Jones et al., 1991; Mathias et al., 1998; Murphy et al., 2004; Murphy et al., 2002; Tchanturia et al., 2002; Tchanturia et al., 2004a) Design fluency tasks have not been utilised with this clinical group.

Inhibition: Response inhibition tasks provide information with regards to cognitive impulsivity or 'disinhibition', typically requiring individuals to inhibit prepotent responses, as seen in the 'Go-No-Go' and the 'Stop' test. Only one published study appears to have utilised such a task with an AN sample (Ohrmann et al., 2004). However, whilst reporting that the participants with AN displayed poorer performance in each neuropsychological test compared to controls, actual data was not given, thus neither the degree of deficit or the specific area of impairment in this task can be determined. The Matching Familiar Figures Task has been used as a measure of cognitive response style, specifically assessing impulsive (poor inhibition) and reflective styles. In the two studies that have utilised this task with AN samples, the performance of participants with the restricting sub-type of AN has been suggestive of a reflective cognitive response style, as indicated by making few mistakes but with longer reaction times (Kaye, Bastiani, & Moss, 1995; Toner, Garfinkel, & Garner, 1987). In comparison, individuals with the binge-purge subtype of AN appear to be more cognitively impulsive as indicated by the opposite response pattern, making inaccurate responses with short reaction times, thus endorsing the distinction between subtypes (Toner et al., 1987).

Planning: Very little work has specifically investigated planning skills in AN. The ability to 'plan' involves identifying and organising individual steps and materials required to achieve a goal. Using the Tower of London task, Seed et al., (2000) did not find any evidence of dysfunction in this executive function.

Decision making: A novel area of research relates to decision making skills in AN (Cavedini et al., 2004; Tchanturia, Uher, Liao, Campbell, & Treasure, in progress). Using the Gambling task (Bechara, Damasio, Damasio, & Anderson, 1994) participants with AN have shown impairment in decision making as indicated by the inability to balance immediate rewards against long-term negative consequences (Cavedini et al., 2004). Our own findings are in line with Cavedini et al., (2004), with AN participants performing significantly worse than controls as indicated by poor strategy use, poor learning over the duration of the task and the accumulation of greater losses, (Tchanturia et al., in progress).

Studies Using Psychiatric Control Groups

Four of the identified studies investigating neuropsychological functioning in AN participants have used psychiatric control groups (other than BN) for comparative purposes. Whilst a number of methodological limitations are relevant for these studies which may explain the inconsistencies in the results reported, they highlight both similarities and differences in neuropsychological functioning across psychiatric disorders.

Intelligence: AN Participants performed better in standard intelligence tests than a mixed psychiatric control group (Blanz et al., 1997).

Attention: A selective impairment in the Symbol Digit Learning Task was found for AN participants compared to three comparative groups; individuals with clinical depression, diabetes or healthy controls (Wit, Ryan and Hsu, 1985).

Set shifting (executive function): Fox (1981) reported that an AN sample had a similar degree of deficit in mental flexibility (measured using the TMT – part B) as a mixed psychiatric control group. However using the same task, the results reported by Murphy et al., (2004), suggest that impaired performance is selective to the diagnosis of OCD as no deficits were apparent in either the AN or BN samples under study.

Memory and Learning: Murphy et al., (2004) reported similar deficits between AN and OCD participants in a Conditional Associative Learning (CAL) Task. Both groups showed selective impairment in learning conditional associations with emotionally neutral stimuli, providing evidence in support of the hypothesis that a common neurobiological dysfunction involving the prefrontal cortex may be involved in these two disorders (Hollander, 1993). This study highlights how the use of clinical controls may help advance theory with regards to the pathogenesis of disorder.

The Effect of Weight Gain on Neuropsychology: Longitudinal Studies

Twelve studies have used a longitudinal design in order to investigate the effect of weight gain on cognitive functions in AN, thus trying to delineate state and trait factors of illness. Again, the results across studies are contradictory, with conflicting reports as to whether improved nutrition enhances neuropsychological performance. The majority of studies that have retested AN participants upon significant weight gain or end of treatment/hospital discharge indicate that at some deficits seem to ameliorate with improved nutritional status. The most consistent improvements in cognition reported across studies concern attention, speed of information processing and problem solving (Kingston et al., 1996; Kohlmeyer, Lehmkuhl, & Poutska, 1983; Lauer et al., 1999; Moser et al., 2003; Szmukler et al., 1992) indicating that neuropsychological dysfunction may be resolved in this clinical group. However these significant gains may not be global, for example Kingston et al., (1996) highlight persistent impairment in memory and visuospatial processing domains amongst individuals who show improvement in attentional capacity. The studies of Green et al., (1996), Grunwald et al., (2002) and Tchanturia et al., (2004b) suggest that deficits in recall, reaction time and motor speed, somatosensory processing and set shifting respectively are not affected by weight gain. Whilst it may be tempting to suggest that these deficits may represent enduring features of disorder, it is important to note that the mean participant BMI's are still in the AN range in two of these studies (Grunwald et al., 2001; Green et al., 1996) and just below what may be considered a 'normal healthy range' (i.e. BMI 19-25) in the remaining study (Tchanturia, 2004b). Thus it remains to be seen whether task performance in such cognitive domains would improve with further weight restoration into a healthy range. Gillberg et al.,

(1994; 1996) found the persistence of dysdiadochokinesis alongside poor performance on the object assembly task (visuo-spatial processing) following weight recovery well into the healthy range. Analyses of inter-individual performance with weight gain, involving the investigation of deficit scores, support the idea that some neuropsychological deficits are independent of illness state. Hamsher et al., (1981) found that at post treatment, having achieved a normal weight for age and height, 60% of the AN sample still displayed at least one cognitive impairment. Furthermore, persistent deficits in learning tasks and equivalent numbers of cognitive deficits found amongst AN participants before and after weight gain have also been found (Kingston et al., 1996). In contrast to these studies highlighting areas of impairment, Bradley et al., (1997) did not find evidence of cognitive impairment at baseline and in follow up tests the AN group performed better than the controls in a visuo-spatial and an attention task. It is apparent that this area of investigation requires much further consideration, with studies following participants from acute illness state into full weight restoration and long-term recovery.

Studies Conducted at 'Recovered' States'

An alternative way to investigate state effects of illness is with a cross sectional design which compares individuals in an acute phase of illness to those who have 'recovered' from the disorder. There are methodological issues which may question the validity of such designs. Questions exist as to what actually constitutes 'recovery' and as to whether those who achieve recovery are representative of the ED population as a whole, or whether the fact that these individuals are able to restore and maintain their weight suggest that they consist of a separate subgroup with 'atypical' AN. Never-the-less cross sectional studies are less costly and easier to conduct than longitudinal approaches and may give initial clues as to which features of disorder are independent of the nutritional status of participants. Six studies incorporating such a design were uncovered in the literature search. Whilst Jones et al., (1991) reported subtle neuropsychological dysfunction in individuals in an acute illness state, long-term recovered AN participants, operationalised as having maintained a weight restored status for at least six months prior to participation, did not show dysfunctional performance in any domain under investigation. In comparison, three studies conducted by our group (Tchanturia et al., 2002; 2004b; Holliday et al., in press) have highlighted the persistence of deficits in cognitive and perceptual set shifting abilities in long-term recovered individuals, leading to the suggestion that these features could represent stable traits of disorder and as such may play a role in the vulnerability towards the development of AN. The criteria for recovered status in the latter three studies were more stringent, requiring participants to have fulfilled the criteria for AN in the past but having maintained a normal weight (BMI 19-24) with regular menstruation for at least a year and to have normal eating patterns.

SUMMARY OF AN LITERATURE

In summary of the existing literature, it appears that some cognitive dysfunction has been reported across each neuropsychological domain highlighted, with the exception of 'intelligence'. Problems in attention processing, which globally indicate increased susceptibility to interference, can have detrimental effects on other processing skills yet deficits have been reported which appear to be independent of this potential confounder. There appears to be a consensus in the literature that AN is associated with problems relating to reactive flexibility (set shifting) in the presence of in-tact spontaneous flexibility (fluency). Further work is required in the other areas of executive functioning before the true nature of executive dysfunction may be determined. It is important to note that anomalous cognitive function may not just result in deficits but also have beneficial effects as highlighted in the visuo-spatial domain, a significant factor to consider in treatment planning. Problems concerning flexibility do not appear to be specific to AN, neither does hyperarousal toward emotionally relevant stimuli. The identification of common features across psychiatric disorders give clues with regards to the aetiological processes involved in AN. Whilst severe emaciation is considered detrimental to cognitive function, it may be concluded from both longitudinal and cross-sectional studies that at least some cognitive deficits associated with AN may be state independent. It has yet to be determined as to whether persistent anomalous function is a 'scar' of the illness or indicative of enduring biological traits.

Chapter 4

Review of BN Literature

Few studies have focused exclusively on the neuropsychological function of individuals with BN. The following review section concentrates on the results from studies which have compared cognitive function in BN to that of healthy control samples.

Attention

The consistent reports of impaired vigilance (sustained attention) in BN by Laessle et al., (1989; 1990; 1992), suggest that BN participants have poor interference control. These results are in contrast to the preserved vigilance function reported by Jones et al., (1991).

The majority of studies investigating speed of information processing in BN, using tasks such as the TMT – part A and the Symbol Digit Modalities Test (SDMT), have highlighted performance in line with healthy control groups (Beatty, Wonderlich, Staton, & Ternes, 1990; Murphy et al., 2004; 2002). However in one study, BN participants performed faster and made more errors than controls in the SDMT, thus demonstrating a response preference for speed over accuracy (Ferraro, Wonderlich, & Jocic, 1997).

Memory and Learning

Divergent reports have been made regarding the efficacy of short-term or working memory processing in BN. Again the majority of studies indicate performances in line with healthy controls (Galderisi et al., 2003; Jones et al., 1991; Murphy et al., 2002) whilst Ferraro et al., (1997) and Beatty et al., (1990) reported that BN participants were poorer at immediate free recall tasks. Using tests of delayed recall and recognition, no problems in long-term memory were found by Beatty et al., (1990).

Unlike those with AN, BN participants performed equally as well as controls on CAL tasks with neutral and disorder specific stimuli (Murphy et al., 2002; 2004). Galderisi et al., highlighted that a sample of individuals with EDs (including participants with BN) were slower in incidental learning and made less error in CAL tasks with external feedback.

Motor Function

One study has suggested that BN participants show problems in the motor domain, performing slower than controls in a simple drawing task used as an assessment of motor processing in the Luria-Nebraska Clinical Scales (McKay, Humphries, Allen, & Clawson, 1986).

Haptic Tasks: Using a haptic illusion task, Tchanturia et al., (2001; 2004a) report than BN participants display anomalous haptic processing, through greater susceptibility to illusion.

Visuo-Spatial Processing

Using a variety of tasks, visuo-spatial processing appears to be preserved in BN across studies (Jones et al., 1991; Murphy et al., 2002; 2004). It is only in one study that BN participants were found to show problems in this domain, however as acknowledged by the authors, the 'Eckman Faces' task that was used involves emotion processing, thus specific difficulties in this task may not be due to poor visuo-spatial processing, rather insensitivity to emotion could be the cause (Ferraro et al., 1997).

Executive Functions

Set shifting: Using the TMT – part B, the research of Murphy et al., (2002; 2004), suggests that BN participants show reactive flexibility. In accordance, using the same task, Tchanturia et al., (2004a) also found that this clinical group perform as well control participants. However such 'normal' performance was not found across all flexibility measures. Using a battery of cognitive and perceptual flexibility tasks, BN participants showed deficits in the factorial variables entitled 'mental flexibility' and 'perceptual shifting' (Tchanturia et al., 2004a). Furthermore, BN participants have shown deficits in the Wisconsin Card Sorting Test (Ferraro et al., 1997).

FLUENCY

As found in the AN literature, the majority of studies that have utilised verbal fluency measures (letter, category and alternation tasks), suggest that spontaneous fluency is in-tact amongst individuals with BN (Murphy et al., 2002; 2004; Tchanturia et al., 2004a). However, the BN sample tested by Beatty et al., (1990) were found to show selective problems in this domain. BN participants were poorer than controls in the naming of famous people (category fluency task) and made more rule violations in the design fluency task. The authors suggest that poor category naming may be indicative of problems in the ability to initiate appropriate strategies to assist self-generated searches of semantic memory (Beatty et al., 1990).

To our knowledge, no studies have been conducted to specifically investigate the efficacy of Inhibition, Planning or Decision making in BN compared to healthy control samples.

Most studies involving BN participants have compared performance with AN samples, many of which have failed to find frank differences in cognitive function across diagnoses (Galderisi et al., 2003; Laessle et al., 1989; Laessle et al., 1992; Lauer et al., 1999; Touyz, Beumont, & Johnstone, 1986). Rather it appears that the qualitative nature of dysfunction or the characteristic pattern of responding may differ between diagnostic groups (Tchanturia et al., 2001; 2004a). Studies have indicated that compared to AN, BN samples display an impulsive cognitive style as indicated by a speed-accuracy trade off in favour of speed (Kaye et al., 1995), and fluctuating as opposed to rigid response patterns (Tchanturia et al., 2001). One published study has reported the absence of neuropsychological anomalies in BN and AN samples compared to theoretical norms (Touyz et al., 1986) however the range of cognitive functions assessed in this study were limited, focusing mainly on intellectual and academic abilities, which typically are not found to differ between ED and healthy control groups.

Longitudinal Studies

With regards to potential state effects of illness on cognitive functioning in BN, the evidence is severely limited. Only one study followed up participants and retested them after a period seven months, during which time they received treatment (Lauer et al., 1999). The authors reported improved performance in attention and problem solving tasks, in parallel with a reduction in the therapeutic outcome variable (frequency of binges). However regression analyses indicated that neuropsychological measures did not predict improvement in BN symptomatology.

Studies Using Psychiatric Control Groups

Three studies have compared the performance of individuals with BN to a psychiatric control group, investigating specificity of cognitive dysfunction across disorders.

Intelligence: BN Participants performed better in standard intelligence tests than a mixed psychiatric control group (Blanz et al., 1997).

Memory and learning: Beatty et al., (1990), found impaired performance in learning and recalling lists of unrelated words to be general across the disorders of BN and major depression. Murphy et al., (2004) reported superior performance by BN participants compared to those with OCD in a CAL task using emotionally neutral stimuli. Performance was similar across groups with disease specific stimuli.

Fluency: Poor performance in a name generation task was similar amongst participants with BN or major depression, whilst excessive rule violations in the design fluency tasks was specifically associated with the diagnosis of BN (Beatty et al., 1990).

Summary of BN Literature

Altogether, the review of existing literature implies that BN could be associated with dysfunction in cognitive functions relating to inhibitory control; encompassing the ability to process information selectively and flexibly, inhibiting inappropriate or irrelevant stimuli and behavioural responses. Examples of this highlighted in the literature include poor vigilance, the preference for speed over accuracy in certain tasks, increased rule violations and fluctuating response

styles. The presence of such cognitive deficits are in accordance with clinical observations and the vast personality and behavioural literature which pertain to high levels of behavioural impulsivity in this clinical group.

Chapter 5

COMBINING NEUROPSYCHOLOGY WITH DIRECT EXPLORATION OF THE BRAIN

STRUCTURE AND FUNCTION

Some work has sought to explore whether the anomalies of brain structure reported in AN and BN are related to functional impairment. Correlational studies have indicated that cerebral atrophy as measured with computed tomography (CT) and magnetic resonance imaging (MRI) has little association with cognitive function. Laessle et al., (1989) reported no relationship between ventricular size and vigilance performance amongst AN and BN participants. Using participants with AN, Kingston et al., (1996) found non- significant trends between enlarged ventricles and poor performance in cognitive flexibility tasks whilst Palazidou, Robinson and Lishman, (1990) highlighted a specific association between poor performance in a symbol-digit task and enlarged cerebrospinal fluid space. This research would suggest that cerebral atrophy does not have severe or global consequences for neuropsychological processes.

'ON-LINE' INVESTIGATION

Technological advances have allowed more detailed and specialized investigations to be conducted into the relationship between brain function and cognition. Using magnetic resonance spectroscopy with AN participants, a recent study highlighted that cognitive impairments are associated with cerebral metabolism (Ohrman et al,. 2004). Specifically, poor divided attention was associated with cell pathology in the dorso-lateral prefrontal cortex. The incorporation of electrophysiological investigation in neuropsychological studies have indicated anomalous cortical functioning in the right hemisphere during the performance of non-verbal tasks (Bradley et al., 1997; Grunwald et al., 2001), even in the absence of frank performance deficit (Bradley et al., 1997). Dodin and Nandrino, (2003), concluded that their electrophysiological recordings of brain activity during visual recognition tasks with AN participants were indicative of non-specific hyperarousal, resulting in "a bias toward a controlled processing mode" involving "systematically allocating a high level of attentional resources, impeding appropriate selective processing of relevant information," (Dodin and Nandrino, 2003, p. 306).

Chapter 6

Methodological Considerations Applicable to Neuropsychological Literature

As highlighted in the review above, whilst providing insight into potential areas of cognitive dysfunction, the neuropsychological data that exists for EDs is somewhat unclear. The lack of consensus across studies may be explained by a number of methodological limitations that are inherent in this literature, thus restricting the conclusions that may be derived. A specifically salient limitation relates to poor reporting of participant characteristics. Important information with regards to clinical status, medication and medical history (especially neurological) are often not reported, preventing the investigation of potential confounding variables. These issues are discussed in the following section accordingly.

Sample Characteristics and Recruitment Bias

A major limitation of the current literature pertains to the heterogeneous nature of the samples under study, a problem relevant for both clinical and control groups. Particular concerns relate to diagnostic issues which are discussed in more detail in the following subsection of this chapter. Further limitations exist with regards to the populations that have been studied in previous research. Selection bias, involving the reliance on participants receiving treatment for their ED, restricts the extent to which research findings can be generalised to the ED population as a whole. Fairburn and Harrison, (2003) highlight that the majority of individuals with BN do not seek treatment. Furthermore, the individuals who receive specialist help for their ED maybe selective of the total population, with an over-representation of patients with additional features such as anxiety, depression and personality disorder, especially those who engage in substance abuse and/or self harm, (Paul, Schroeter, Dahme, & Nutzinger, 2002). Similarly, questions arise with regards to the representative nature of 'control' populations which are often found to consist solely of undergraduate students or hospital staff, especially as maladaptive eating patterns have been found to be pervasive in higher education populations (Mintz & Betz, 1988). Most studies employ healthy control groups for comparative purposes, where as psychiatric control groups are also required to investigate the specificity of any potential dysfunction. Such understanding is essential if we are to evaluate the clinical utility of neuropsychological testing in EDs.

Diagnostic Issues and the Question of Subtypes

Diagnostic issues may contribute towards the confusing and sometimes contradictory literature. DSM IV recognises two sub-types of anorexia nervosa based on eating pathology (American Psychiatric Association, 1994). Patients with 'restricting type' (RAN) control their weight through food restriction alone, where as those with 'binge-eating/purging type' (BPAN) also engage in binge-eating with compensatory purging behaviours to reduce weight gain. The validity of these subtypes of AN have been endorsed in the vast personality literature, with reports of those with BPAN anorexia displaying more impulsive personality styles and behaviours compared to those with pure RAN (Claes, Vandereycken, & Vertommen, 2002; DaCosta & Halmi, 1992). Neurophysiological differences have also been shown to exist. Individuals with binge-purge anorexia showed different patterns of regional cerebral blood flow when imagining food than restrictors (Naruo et al., 2000). These findings implicate the potential for neuropsychological differences to exist across subtypes, yet there is little data upon which to draw conclusions. Thirty seven percent of the reviewed studies were published before the introduction of DSM-IV (APA, 1994) and the move to split patients into subtypes. Furthermore, in the few studies in which AN subtypes were taken into account, the results are inconsistent. Strupp et al., (1986) and Tchanturia (2004a; 2004b) did not find any differences in cognitive style between the subgroups, where as Toner et al., (1987) reported that their BPAN group showed a more impulsive response style than their RAN group. However the reliance on retrospective diagnoses in the later study is not ideal. Most recently, Cavadini et al., (2004), report differences in the pattern of decision making impairments seen across the subtypes of AN that were independent of other clinical variables such as nutritional status, severity and duration of illness. Where diagnostic subtypes are mentioned in the description of participant characteristics, the majority of studies report the inclusion of individuals from both groups in their AN sample (Pallanti, Quercioli, Zaccara, Ramacciotti, & Arnetoli, 1998; Tchanturia et al., 2004a; Tchanturia et al., 2004b) and it is assumed that this is true for the remaining studies in which subtypes are not mentioned. RAN is the most homogeneous and 'pure' of the ED diagnostic groups (Kaye et al., 2000), perhaps making the research in which investigates RAN as a distinct sample, the most reliable (Fassino et al., 2002; Green et al., 1996; Kaye et al., 1995; Tchanturia et al., 2001).

Whilst there may be a clear argument for the acknowledgement of different AN subtypes in neuropsychological studies, caveats related this also exist in the literature. It has been suggested that rather than representing different sub-types, 'restricting' and 'binge-purging' symptoms characterize different phases of illness (Eddy et al., 2002). AN sub-groups were found not to differ on outcome variables such as time to recovery, relapse or mortality rates. Furthermore, subtype diagnoses appeared to be transient, as the cross over rate from RAN to BPAN was high; the incidence of regular binge-purging increasing as the duration of the follow up increased. Movement across diagnostic categories is found to occur frequently in EDs, typically from AN into BN and 'eating disorder not otherwise specified' (EDNOS) (Fairburn & Harrison, 2003). This idea is elaborated upon in a transdiagnostic model of EDs (Fairburn, Cooper, & Shafran, 2003), which proposes that the shared clinical features across the disorders and the movement of patients between diagnostic states are suggestive of common maintaining processes, questioning the utility of the current classification system.

The fact that ED diagnoses can be unstable can cause difficulty for the utility of categorical diagnoses and analyses based upon these. In order to uncover true phenotypic traits associated with specific disorders, it may be necessary for detailed symptom histories to be incorporated into 'lifetime' diagnoses, ensuring that an individual's full range of pathology is taken into account. All analyses reported in the existing literature were conducted using current categorical diagnoses (providing relevant information with regards to current illness state) with the exception of one (Leassle et al., 1990), whose results perhaps highlight the importance of combining current and historical symptomatology to produce lifetime diagnoses when investigating phenotypic traits. A differential pattern of information processing was uncovered for participants with current BN who had a history of AN compared to those who had not experienced AN in the past. Those who had AN prior to BN displayed more rigid and cautious response styles compared to those with pure BN diagnoses, which appears to be in line with characteristic personality features of AN (Lilenfeld et al., 2001). Thus it may be that diagnostic groupings based on current symptomatology alone may be contributing to the conflicting results due to the heterogeneity of participants within them. Inconsistent results may be a product of underlying differences in the populations under study despite similarities in their current symptoms experienced. An obvious problem in assigning 'lifetime diagnoses' is the fact that an individual's symptoms may still change in the future. It has been indicated that diagnostic change in AN typically occurs within three years from the initial onset of disorder (Bulik et al., 1997), therefore by limiting the inclusion of participants to those who have been ill for three or more years, it is likely that major diagnostic change will have occurred and a more representative symptom profile may be determined. This strategy has been employed by the Price Foundation (Kaye et al., 2000).

Study Design and Statistical Analyses

Design flaws are present in the research reviewed. Studies have been conducted with small samples sizes, limiting the power of the study to detect group differences and increasing the risk of type II error (favouring the null hypothesis when the alternative hypothesis is true). When reviewing the current literature, it is important to take into account the statistical methods employed to determine how reliable and valid the conclusions derived may be. Ideally, raw data should be explored to determine as to whether it reaches the requirements necessary for the use of parametric tests, if not non-parametric tests need to be employed or data transformed to fit the normal distribution. Multiple comparison testing should be avoided (e.g. the use of multiple t-tests to conduct a number of between group comparisons) and when unavoidable, appropriate correction procedures should be utilised (e.g. Bonferroni correction procedure for multiple comparisons), which adjusts the alpha level used to determine statistical significance. These procedures help to reduce the risk of type 1 error (accepting the alternative hypothesis when the null hypothesis is true). In addition to the popular adherence of reporting alpha levels as an indication of statistical significance, the importance of conducting power analyses and reporting confidence intervals and effect sizes to evaluate outcome in neuropsychological research has been made explicit (Bezeau & Graves, 2001).

Participant groups should be matched according to demographics to reduce the possibility of confounding variables, and where differences exist, analyses need to take these covariates into account (e.g. through the use of ANCOVA). Similarly, relationships between comorbid psychopathology and the dependent variables of interest should be explored. If significant associations exist, the levels of comorbidity which differ amongst individuals need to be taken into account to ensure that group differences are not attributable to the presence of additional psychopathology. Few studies have used or reported the use of such rigorous statistical methodologies discussed here, thus raising questions with regards to how robust the findings are.

TASK IMPURITY AND SENSITIVITY

The methodological problem relating to test impurity has already been alluded to in this chapter. Many neuropsychological tests are multidimensional, requiring the efficacy of a number of cognitive components for accurate performance, the specific functions involved being very hard to isolate and measure. There is especially great overlap amongst tests used to measure the cognitive constructs of attention, memory and executive functions. Thus it is not completely apparent as to which of these constructs deficits should be attributed to in the presence of anomalous performance. The multiple components involved in test performance can explain why the same tasks have been used across studies to assess diverse cognitive domains or 'constructs'. For example the same task may be referred to by different research groups as a measurement of attention or executive functioning, resulting in divergent research findings and the lack of replication across studies. This methodological problem relates to the more fundamental issue of poor construct validity, with few investigations into the underlying variables of test performance (Miyake et al., 2000). These issues have been taken into account in the work of our research group. Tchanturia et al., (2004a) explored the latent variables underlying performance in their test battery using exploratory factor analysis, indicating that a battery purported to investigate cognitive flexibility comprised of the following factors 'simple alternation', 'mental flexibility', 'perseveration' and 'category shifting'. This test battery has been applied in a number of studies, resulting in the replication of data and providing a solid foundation of knowledge on which to base conclusions (Tchanturia et al, 2001; 2002; 2004a, 2004b; Holliday et al., in press).

As well as reservations pertaining to the purity of cognitive functions measured, questions can be raised as to the sensitivity of the neuropsychological tests and their utility in psychiatric populations (Tchanturia et al., in press). Many of the tests employed were historically designed for use with populations who have experienced severe head injuries or trauma to the brain to explore the effects of gross brain lesions. Whilst various psychiatric disorders are associated with anomalous brain structure and processing pathways, such extreme anatomical damage or abnormality is not characteristic or commonly found. It is especially questionable as to whether these tests are sensitive enough to pick up the more subtle deficits expected to be associated with EDs. Evidence to suggest that the task insensitivity may be a problem in the current ED literature can be seen in the work of Bradley et al., (1997) and more recently Dodin and Nandrino, (2003). Both research groups have identified anomalous/inefficient information processing in response to cognitive tasks using electrophysiological measures of brain activity (event-related potentials), this being in the absence of clear deficits in neuropsychological test performance in the former study.

Potential Confounding Variables:

i) History of Head Trauma

As previously discussed in this chapter, pregnancy and birth complications (PBCs), including prematurity, can result in anomalous brain development or damage. As an increased risk of anorexia has been associated with pre and perinatal factors, it would appear important to investigate such variables as potential confounds in the neuropsychological literature, yet few do. Additionally, not all studies have reported as to whether their participant samples may include individuals with a history of head injury or neurological disorder, important variables to take into account and detail when investigating brain function. Four studies have acknowledged PBCs in their design, however the reliance on self report/maternal report of PBCs may limit the reliability of this data due to problems associated with retrospective reporting such as memory loss or bias. Mathias and Kent (1998) calculated that 22% of their AN sample had a history of PBCs or head injury, comparable rates to that of their control sample. Kingston et al., (1996) reported that 12% of their AN sample had possible perinatal injury. Neither study investigated these potential confounding variables further. Palazidou et al., (1990) excluded participants if there was the possibility that they had experienced perinatal injury, whilst Hamsher et al., (1981) correlated the number of PBCs reported with number of cognitive deficits following treatment, finding no significant relationship. Eleven studies explicitly state that they have excluded participants if they have any history of head injury or neurological illness (Beatty et al., 1990; Cavedini et al., 2004; Holliday et al., in press; McKay et al., 1986, Moser et al., 2003; Murphy et al., 2002; 2004; Ohrman et al., 2004, Palazidou et al., 1990; Pallanti et al., 1998; Szmuckler et al., 1992; Tchanturia et al, 2004a).

On a related theme, the minority of research studies conducted refer to alcohol consumption and substance abuse in the selection criteria of their participants. Again these are factors which may be related to anomalous brain structure and function and thus potential confounders for the neuropsychological literature. Eight studies state the exclusion of participants who have a history of alcohol and substance abuse (Cavedini et al., 2004; Galderisi et al.,2003; Kingston et al., 1996, Mathias and Kent, 1998; Palazidou et al., 1990; Pallanti et al., 1998; Pieters et al., 2003; Szmuckler et al., 1992) whilst the remaining studies do not report on these important variables.

ii) Psychotropic Medication

Current medication at the time of testing has not been systematically reported in the literature. Antidepressant medications including selective serotonin reuptake inhibitors are often used by individuals with EDs, especially those with BN (Kaye, Klump, Frank, & Strober, 2000). Modification of serotonin can affect cognition (Lucki, 1998), so this could be an important confounder. Thirteen studies ensured ED participants were medication free for at least two weeks prior to testing (please refer to table 2). Four studies reported that a subset of their ED participants were taking psychotropic medication in the form of antidepressants at the time of testing (Kingston et al., 1996; Mathias and Kent, 1998; Murphy et al., 2002; Tchanturia et al., 2004a) of which two investigated the possible effects of medication on performance by excluding those taking it and rerunning the analyses (Kingston et al., 1996; Tchanturia et al., 2004a). Both studies found that the results did not change when those participants on medication were excluded.

The potential effects of medication on cognitive function have not been investigated to any real degree in the ED literature, compounded by the fact that many studies do not report on the medication status of their participants. This is an extremely important area of future study if we are to understand the true neurobiological correlates of EDs.

iii) Illness Severity

Research into AN typically uses an individual's body mass index (weight in kg/height in metres squared) as an indicator of illness severity, with lower BMIs indicating the most chronic cases. This is also true of the neuropsychological literature. Whilst not all research has sought to investigate the relationship between cognitive function and degree of emaciation, those that have reveal inconsistent results. Nutritional status as indicated by current BMI was not found to be associated with neuropsychological impairment in the majority of studies (Bayless et al., 2002; Bowers, 1994; Cavadini et al., 2004; Green et al., 1996; Grunwald et al., 2001; Fassino et al., 2002; Lawrence et al., 2003; Mathias and Kent, 1998; Moser et al., 2003; Murphy et al., 2002; Tchanturia, 2004a; Witt et al., 1985) and yet low BMI was found to be specifically related to poor cognitive flexibility and memory functions by Kingston et al., (1996) and poor maze learning by Szmuckler et al., (1992). Other indicators of severity have been overlooked in many studies, such as duration of illness, number of hospital admissions and comorbidity. Few studies have investigated the relationship between these variables and neuropsychological function. Kingston et al., (1996) found a positive relationship between chronicity of illness (based upon number of hospital admissions) and the tendency towards impairment in flexibility/inhibition functions. Whilst reporting that levels of severity or psychopathology (as determined by self report symptom and attitude measures, using the Eating Disorder Inventory) were unrelated to cognitive performance, Fassino et al., (2002) highlighted a relationship between poor body image and reduced performance in the WCST, a measure of cognitive flexibility.

Severity markers such as BMI and hospital admission are redundant in the study of BN, as weight change is typically unremarkable in this group and reduced medical risk allows treatment to usually be applied in an outpatient setting. Therefore severity is often determined by the frequency of binge/purge behaviour and levels of psychopathology as indicated by self report measures. Again, amongst studies that have investigated this, cognitive function appears to be independent of symptom severity (Bowers, 1994; Laessle, Bossert, Hank, Hahlweg, & Pirke, 1990; Laessle et al., 1992). Interestingly Laessle et al (1990) did find some illness related factors to be associated with neuropsychological performance with a group of BN participants. Those who had a past history of AN and individuals with biological indicators suggesting high levels of starvation displayed more problems in the tasks employed. This would appear to suggest that a period of starvation may be related to cognitive dysfunction, leaving a 'scar' in neuropsychological function, or it may be that this group represents a different illness sub-type. To our knowledge no study as yet has replicated such findings.

iv) Comorbidities: Disorders of Affect and Anxiety

On a related theme, it possible that the information processing deficits displayed by individuals with EDs may be related to secondary pathologies commonly found amongst patients, characteristically disorders of affect and anxiety (O'Brien & Vincent, 2003). Again, not all studies have taken these potential confounding factors into account.

Depression: The existing literature clearly suggests that cognitive function is unrelated to current mood status in both AN and BN (Beatty et al; Green et al,. 1995; Jones et al., 1991; Kingston et al., 1996; Laessle et al., 1990; Lawrence et al,. 2003; Szmuckler et al., 1992; Tchanturia et al., 2001; 2002; 2004a). McDowell et al., (2003) specifically investigated this with a large sample of AN patients and multiple measures of depression, again finding no evidence to suggest that cognitive function is related to levels of depression.

Anxiety: The literature regarding the relationship between cognitive function and anxiety in eating disorders is not so clear cut. There is some evidence to suggest that high levels of anxiety are related to performance deficits in neuropsychological tests (Jones et al., 2001), yet this has not been consistently found across studies (Green et al., 1996; Lawrence et al., 2003). It has been suggested that the anxious, hyperaroused state typical of AN, biases cognitive style towards a controlled information processing mode, which requires “a high level of attentional resources, impeding appropriate selective processing of relevant information” (Dodin and Nandrino, p. 306).

OCD: Obsessive-compulsive disorder is an anxiety disorder frequently found to be comorbid in EDs, AN in particular, (Lifetime OCD comorbidity rates 9% - 63% in AN: 0% - 43% in BN; (Speranza, Corcos, Godart, Jeammet, & Flament, 2001). The large number of neuropsychological studies conducted in OCD have generally indicated that this disorder may be associated with deficits within the realms of memory, attention and executive function (for a review see Kuelz, Hohagen and Voderholzer, 2004). Despite the many psychopathological similarities and high rates of comorbidity between disorders, the relationship between obsessive-compulsive symptomatology and cognitive functioning in EDs has not been systematically explored in the current literature. Only two studies have investigated OCD symptomatology and neurocognitive function in EDs; Pallanti et al., (1998) found that alterations in smooth pursuit eye movement were related to the severity of OCD symptomatology in their AN participants, whilst using a self-report measure of obsessive-compulsive behaviour as a covariate, Tchanturia et al (2002; 2004a) found that group differences in neuropsychological function remained the same and thus could not be attributed to the presence of OC symptoms. The existence of frank OCD has not been taken into account when explaining the results of neuropsychological studies in EDs. It would be of particular interest to investigate as to whether those with comorbid OCD display a profile of cognitive performance in line with that reported in the OCD literature. This appears to be especially relevant as in the only comparative study to date, AN and OCD participants were found to show the same performance in a conditional associative learning task, leading the authors to suggest that the data is reflective of "common neurobiological and neuropsychological dysfunctions with reference to frontal-subcortical abnormalities" (Murphy et al., 2004, p. 197) across disorders.

v) Neuroendocrine Changes

Functional changes to biological systems are observed in AN and BN, including disturbance to the neuroendocrine system. As endocrine abnormalities, involving cortisol and neuroactive steroids involved in the HPA axis are thought to effect cognitive functions (Lupien et al., 1994; Vedhara, Hyde, Gilchrist, Tytherleigh, & Plummer, 2000), four studies to date have investigated as to whether neuropsychological test performance is mediated by neuroendocrine disturbance (Galderisi et al., 2003; Laessle et al., 1992; Seed et al., 2000; 2002). The divergent findings reported may be attributable to the various methods used to measure endocrine levels. Seed et al. (2002; 2000) focused their attention on cortisol levels in individuals with AN, finding no correlation between cortisol and impaired cognitive functioning, which the authors describe as indicating enhanced sensitivity to distraction. In comparison, Laessle et al., (1992) reported that elevated levels of cortisol were in fact associated with poorer performance in a vigilance task. Galderisi et al., (2003) also investigated levels of neuroactive steroids and cognitive function. The neuroendocrine profile indicated hyperactivity of the HPA axis, with elevated cortisol levels being related to poorer performance in incidental learning and elevated neuroactive steroids being associated with enhanced performance in effortful processing. Thus anomalous activity of the HPA axis was associated with both selective impairment and preservation of cognitive functions. It appears that neuroendocrine systems could mediate the relationship between EDs and cognitive function, however, it is not possible to conclude from studies investigating associations between variables that this is the cause of impairment in neuropsychological tasks. Furthermore, the presence of cognitive dysfunction in the absence of anomalous endocrine levels (Seed et al., 2002) or unrelated to these biological systems suggest that either cognitive impairment is attributable to other factors or that current methods of endocrine assessment lack sensitivity to highlight such relationships.

Chapter 7

NEUROPSYCHOLOGY, PERSONALITY AND BEHAVIOUR

PERSONALITY AND BEHAVIOUR IN EDS

Much research into ED phenotypes has focused on personality characteristics. Consistent reports of compulsive, perfectionistic and rigid personality styles have been endorsed for individuals with AN, especially of the restricting subtype (e.g.Vitousek & Manke, 1994; Sohlberg & Strober, 1994). Retrospective and longitudinal studies have highlighted the importance of these characteristics, being present both premorbidly (Anderluh, Tchanturia, Rabe-Hesketh, & Treasure, 2003) and after recovery (Casper, 1990; Srinivasagam et al., 1995). Such results imply that they are stable traits, potentially increasing an individual's vulnerability to disorder and being involved in treatment resistance, symptom maintenance and relapse risk. Indeed personality has been found to act as a persistent and stable risk factor for mental disorder (affective, anxiety, substance dependence and anti-social personality disorders) in a prospective longitudinal study conducted across late adolescence and early adulthood (Krueger, 1999). Impulsive personality characteristics have also been reported in AN (Sohlberg, Norring, Holmgren, & Rosmark, 1989; Askenazy et al., 1998). Whilst compulsive and impulsive traits have been suggested to lie at the opposite ends of the personality dimension 'risk avoidance' (Hollander, 1998), research demonstrates that they are not mutually exclusive (Claes, Vandereyken and Vertommen, 2002). This is further supported by the personality profile typical of BN. Again both perfectionistic and impulsive characteristics have been associated with this diagnostic group (Vitousek and Manke, 1994), with impulsive traits being clear in symptomatology and behaviour (Fahy & Eisler, 1993; Penas-Lledo, Vaz, Ramos, & Waller, 2002)

Exploring the Relationship Between Personality and Cognition

In general, little work has been conducted across psychiatric disorders exploring as to whether there is a link between cognition and personality. Such a link would appear coherent due to the mutual neuroanatomical localisation of function in the frontal lobes (Cummings, 1993). This question has been of importance historically, with Eysenck (1947) associating differences in perceptual style to differences in temperament, " Individuals differ with respect to the length of after-effects of sensory stimulation, and these individual differences are closely related to the individual's temperament" (Eysenck, 1947, p. 154). Recent studies, whilst few in number, have also endorsed the connection between personality and neuropsychological function. Significant relationships between laboratory and personality measures of impulsivity have been reported (Logan, Schachar, & Tannock, 1997; Spinella, 2004; Swann, Bjork, Moeller, & Dougherty, 2002), with one study concluding that an information processing approach "allows us to understand the characteristics of normal and abnormal personalities in terms of underlying cognitive processes" (Logan et al, 1997, p. 64). Links between negative schizotypal personality traits and cognitive deficits have been found in patients with schizophrenia and their first-degree relatives (Laurent et al., 2001). Further research into psychosis has indicated that general personality dimensions are associated with cognitive disturbance, (Cuesta, Peralta, & Zarzuela, 2001) reporting a strong linear association between the two global domains of personality and cognition using canonical correlation analysis ($r=0.68$).

Indirect evidence to suggest a link between personality and cognition may be found in the study of childhood developmental disorders such as ADHD and Autism. Neuropsychological investigations have identified broad phenotypes for these disorders, in which cognitive profiles appear in line with the extreme personality and behavioural traits present. For example, Barkley (1997) suggests that an underlying deficit in response inhibition, as highlighted in numerous neuropsychological tasks, can account for the core features of ADHD; inattention, impulsivity and hyperactivity. 'Weak central coherence' has been posited to be the broad phenotype for autism, manifest in the cognitive and behavioural styles of children with autism and their parents (Briskman, Happe, & Frith, 2001; Happe, Briskman, & Frith, 2001).

Cognitive Performance in AN: An Example of Striving for Perfection and Rule Bound Behaviour?

In accordance with the suggestion that high academic achievement is a consequence of perfectionistic striving rather than elevated IQ, inconsistencies in task performance across diverse neuropsychological assessments may be a consequence of the desire to perform 'correctly'. For example, Galderisi et al., (2003) reported that AN participants were slower and more accurate in their incidental learning and spatial executive tasks. In contrast, Pieters et al., (2003) found their AN sample responded more quickly, with faster reaction times and more errors in a psychomotor task. This apparent paradox may be because AN participants follow the respective requirements of neuropsychological tasks as closely as possible; those used in the Galderisi et al., (2003) study had an emphasis on accuracy of performance where as the drawing tasks in the Pieters et al., (2003) study emphasised the importance of speed. This response style across tasks concords with the typical personality traits seen in this clinical group.

Exploratory Studies in EDs

The suggestion of a link between personality and cognition in EDs is not entirely novel as previous authors have pertained to the fact that associations may be present (Strupp, Weingartner, Kaye, & Gwirtsman, 1986). However, little work has been purposefully done to explore as to whether the characteristic traits highlighted above have information processing parallels, explicitly investigating as to whether biological traits analogous to those relating to personality and behaviour exist. In recent years, the work of our department has focused upon this potential link with current findings indicating that performance in set shifting tasks is associated with childhood perfectionism (Tchanturia et al. 2004b). Furthermore following the methods of Cuesta et al., (2001), these personality and cognitive variables were also strongly related overall (r=0.70, canonical correlation) (Tchanturia, personal communication). The success of this hypothesis driven approach lead us to endorse its use in the future study of neuropsychological processing in EDs.

Chapter 8

UTILISING A HYPOTHESIS DRIVEN APPROACH

A hypothesis testing approach to neuropsychological assessment is utilised in the clinical domain, where tests exploring cognitive functions are selected according to individual strengths and weaknesses. We have exploited this type of approach in our research conducted in the Eating Disorder Research Unit based at the Institute of Psychiatry, London. Neuropsychological tasks have been chosen according to the underlying abilities they are believed to assess and their putative link with personality traits. This experimental based approach has shown efficacy in the quest for delineating neurocognitive systems more specifically and tracking their impairment in AN.

PREVIOUS WORK OF OUR GROUP

Our neuropsychological research has been based around the observation that people with AN show high harm avoidance, inflexibility of thinking and rigid behaviours around eating, with high levels of perfectionism contributing to the disorder as a core feature (Bulik et al., 2003; Lilenfeld et al., 2001; Srinivasagam et al., 1995; Sutandar-Pinnock, Woodside, Carter, Olmsted, & Kaplan, 2003). As discussed in the review of the literature above, neuropsychological studies have highlighted a tendency for individuals with AN to be inflexible on certain cognitive tasks, indicating an inability to change past patterns of thinking. These characteristic features can be conceptualized as difficulties in set-shifting, thus we hypothesized that people with AN would demonstrate this inflexibility in a variety of experimental measures. Our hypothesis has been supported in a series of studies. We began with a simple perceptual test, the Haptic illusion task

(Tchanturia et al., 2001), to clarify whether people with AN would demonstrate set shifting difficulties in the perceptual domain. By conducting a study using both cognitive and perceptual set-shifting tasks, we found that difficulties were not restricted to the perceptual domain and furthermore, were evident in some individuals long-term recovered from AN (Tchanturia et al., 2002). Subsequently, we developed a broader battery of set-shifting tasks, which we used in a larger sample of women with EDs to explore the specificity of our findings. Broad set-shifting difficulties were evident in individuals with acute AN and following weight restoration (Tchanturia et al., 2004b). Intriguingly, a separate comparison between acute AN and long term recovered patients, showed enhanced performance at recovery in only a subset of set-shifting tasks: it is possible that these tasks measure state related neuropsychological impairment or alternatively may represent those that are illness-related irrespective of weight gain. We have extended this research, conducting the same neuropsychological tests in sister pairs discordant for AN and the data suggests that difficulties in some set shifting tasks are shared by the healthy sisters of those with AN, thus introducing the possibility that this feature may be part of the endophenotype (Holliday et al., in press). Whilst the results using our broad 'set shifting battery' have typically been reported as indicative of deficits in cognitive flexibility, we have recently proposed an alternative hypothesis to account for why deficits may be seen in selective set-shifting tasks (Holliday et al., in press). Deficits have typically been found in tasks that involve a learning component, in which the shifting of cognitive/perceptual set requires the extinction of a previously learned response. Thus cognitive dysfunction in this domain could be related to problems in the process of extinction rather than flexibility per se. This hypothesis corresponds with a novel maintenance theory for AN (Strober, 2004), involving the resistance of fear conditioning to processes of extinction. The putative link between ED and a dysfunction of extinction processes is one of the topics under investigation in our current work.

Chapter 9

CONCLUSION

To review the literature as a whole, it would appear that EDs are associated with some anomalous cognitive functioning extending across many domains, including attention, memory, executive functions, motor control and visuo-spatial processing. However is it also apparent that there is not a general or global deficit in information processing. Intellectual ability in this clinical group has consistently been found to be in the normal-high range and it is most often the case that selective deficits have been reported in the presence of preserved, and in some cases superior function in other cognitive domains. It is also clear from the literature that not all individuals with EDs display neuropsychological dysfunction. A number of studies conducting between group analyses do not indicate differential performance in tasks, whilst examination of the results demonstrate that ED samples are more variable in performance. This heightened variability have lead some to conduct inter-individual comparisons which explore deficit scores. Using such analyses, sub-groups of participants have been reported to show defective functioning, performing at a level significantly below average group scores (e.g. Bowers, 1994; Hamsher et al., 1981; Kingston et al., 1996; Palazidou et al., 1990; Szmuckler et al., 1992;). Lauer et al., (1999) suggested that the contradictory nature of the current literature may explained by the inclusion of different numbers of individuals with deficits across studies. However, the value of deficit score analyses are currently limited as they are often conducted without clear hypotheses in mind and it remains to be determined as to whether those individuals displaying cognitive deficits could represent separate neurobiological sub-types of ED. Ferraro et al., (1997) highlight a more methodologically sound approach to exploring performance variability in neuropsychological tasks. By providing a clear hypotheses and utilising statistical measures of variance, the authors suggest that increases in performance variability are suggestive of cognitive dysfunction and thus advocate the use of exploring individual differences within samples.

The neuropsychological correlates of anorexia nervosa are not totally clear yet. Recurrent themes in the literature or the most consistent results relate to: hyper arousal in AN; anomalous attentional processing, including cognitive biases in the processing of illness related stimuli; selective executive function deficits, specifically problems in set shifiting tasks; the putative link between cognitive function and personality styles; and on a similar theme, the potential for the involvement of common neurobiological traits/brain-behaviour pathways in EDs and OCD, possibly playing a role in their shared phenomenology. The pattern of neuropsychological performance displayed is consistent with irregular functioning of the frontal lobes. Indeed the anomalous information processing highlighted appears to be in line with the anatomical areas of dysfunction as seen in imaging studies i.e. the orbito-frontal cortex and the dorso-lateral prefrontal cortex (Uher et al 2003; 2004). Also in line with some of the neuroimaging literature are the selective improvements in neuropsychological performance after weight gain in AN. However, as a whole, the literature suggests that cognitive function is independent of psychopathology and malnutrition, further endorsing the possibility that the presence of neuropsychological dysfunction is not simply a consequence of illness state, rather a potential vulnerability trait or aetiological feature of disorder.

Few neuropsychological differences have been made explicit between the diagnoses of AN and BN. As made apparent by the size of the literature reviews above, much more research has been conducted with AN than BN patients. A good deal of the literature based upon neuropsychological functioning in BN is in accordance with deficits pertaining to response inhibition and inhibitory control, in line with symptom features. The research exploring cognitive function between the subtypes of AN has indicated the predominance of similarities rather than differences. Design flaws including the lack of statistical power caused by small sample sizes, may be a contributing factor as to why underlying differences may not have been discovered. However, the utility of the subtypes has been called into question, thus such findings would appear to support this line of reasoning.

Many studies have not adequately controlled for potential confounding variables, making it difficult to draw conclusions regarding the neuropsychological correlates of EDs. Confounders that have been overlooked involve; mixed study populations and control groups, premorbid trauma to the head, neurological disease, participant medication and psychological comorbidity. Failing to provide details concerning the study population limits the generalisability of the research finding. Furthermore clinical populations of people with EDs are heterogenous; with individual differences concerning age of onset, symptomatology, length of illness and treatment history, all of which provide clues concerning the severity of the disorder. Failure to report on the diagnostic methods utilised or the specific symptoms present in the sample tested seriously question the validity of the research results. In general, the poor reporting of sample characteristics has made it difficult to determine whether deficits are linked to the severity of the illness or specific psychopathology associated with a sub-group of suffers. It is imperative that future studies are more diligent in the descriptions of the participants under study. Methodological problems further limit the conclusions that can be derived. Many different paradigms have been used to assess the same cognitive processes, preventing the direct comparison and integration of results across studies. Failing to find significant differences in the cognitive function of psychiatric and control groups could be due to measures not being sensitive enough to detect subtle differences or problems relating to study design, such as small sample sizes and lack of statistical power.

The limitations of previous research could explain the confusing and often contradictory results reported. However, that is not to say that what has been revealed is not of interest or use. The application of neuropsychological techniques to study this clinical group has provided valuable clues concerning cognitive function in AN and BN and a basis upon which to build our understanding. Furthermore the presence of skewed cognitive skills have important therapeutic implications. For example, treatment may need to focus on the remediation of areas in which there is suboptimal performance, and perhaps dampen down dominant processing styles to help individuals to be more adaptive to environmental challenges. Thus the assessment of neuropsychological function may assist in the adaptation of treatment programmes and goals. It is now important to learn from what has already been reported and develop our methodologies to advance our knowledge base.

It is clear from the current review of the literature that there are significant gaps in the research that has been conducted, leaving many questions to be answered (a selection of which are highlighted below) and more exciting research to be conducted. It is of up most importance that future work tries to address the many methodological limitations apparent in the research conducted to date. This will ensure the reliability and validity of the data derived. Once putative neurocorrelates of EDs are established based upon the results of indirect measures of brain function, it would be appropriate to apply more direct and technologically advanced measures of functioning with this clinical group. Before functional imaging techniques can be utilised in the exploration of brain function, the neuropsychological tests which show appropriate sensitivity with this clinical group need to be determined.

Table 1. Neuropsychological tests commonly used in the current literature according to the purported cognitive domain under study.

Cognitive Domain	Abbreviation	Neuropsychological Test
General intellectual ability and premorbid intelligence	NART	National Adult Reading Test
	RSPMT	Raven Standard Progressive Matrices Test
	WAIS (R)	Wechsler Adult Intelligence Scale (Revised)
	WISC (R)	Wechsler Intelligence Scale for Children (Revised)
	WRAT	Wide Range Achievement Test
Executive functions	BMAPS	Bexley Maudsley Automated Psychological Screening
	BMCST	Bexley Maudsley Category Sorting Test
	COWA	Controlled Oral Word Association Test
	DF	Design Fluency
	DLPST	Daily Living Problem Solving Task
	MFFT	Matching Familiar Figures Test
	SCAL / NSCAL	Spatial / Non-spatial Conditional Associative Learning Task.
	TMT	Trail Making Test
	WCST	Wisconsin Card Sorting Test
	SOPT	Self Ordered Pointing Task
Memory	AVLT	Auditory Verbal Learning Task
	BPSTM	Brown-Peterson Short Term Memory
	BSRT	Buschke Selective Reminding Test
	BVRT	Benton Visual Retention Test
	CBTT	Corsi's Block Tapping Task
	HDRS	Hebb's Digit Recurring Sequences
	RFT	Recurring Figures Test
	ROCF	Rey-Osterrieth Complex Figure Test
	WMS (R)	Wechsler Memory Scale (Revised)
	SAT	Semantic Aphasia Test
Attention	BVT	Bakan Vigilance Task
	CPT	Continuous Performance Test
	DAT	Divided Attention Task
	FAT	Focused Attention Task (modified from Eriksen and Eriksen 1974)
	SDLT	The Symbol-Digit Learning Task
	SDMT	The Symbol-Digit Modalities Task
	(T)LCT	(Talland) Letter Cancellation Test
Motor	SRT	Simple Reaction Time
	FT	Finger Tapping

Visual and Auditory Test Batteries	LOT	Judgement of Line Orientation Test
	TST	Titmus Stereo Tests
	CDR:	Cognitive Drug Research computerised assessment system. Immediate and delayed word recall, simple reaction time, choice reaction time, digit vigilance, spatial working memory, memory scanning, word recognition, picture recognition.
	LNNB:	Luria-Nebraska Neuropsychological Battery Scales consist of motor, rhythm, tactile, visual, receptive, expressive, writing, reading, arithmetic, memory, intelligence, pathognomonic (items most sensitive to brain damage), right hemisphere, left hemisphere
	RBANS:	Repeatable Battery for the Asessment of Neuropsychological status (Randolph, 1998) List learning, story memory, figure copy, line orientation, picture naming, semantic fluency, digit span, coding, list recall and recognition, story and figure recall

QUESTIONS REQUIRING FURTHER EXPLORATION

Despite research into the neuropsychological correlates of EDs spanning many years, it appears that few questions have been answered with any clarity. Research has yet to determine as to whether specific neuropsychological traits are in fact associated with EDs and to whether specific relationships exist between cognitive functions and differential ED symptomatology/sub-groups. Further fundamental research needs to clarify as to whether neuropsychological performance is state or trait related and the specificity of dysfunction to EDs as opposed to general psychopathology. Investigating as to whether cognitive function has prognostic impact on the course of illness and treatment response will be of great clinical and theoretical relevance, as would investigating the possibility that differences in cognitive function may be associated with comorbidity, such as the presence of OCD symptoms. On a related theme, exploring the relationship between personality traits and cognitive functions would contribute to our understanding with regards to a biological basis of illness phenotype.

Table 2. Neuropsychological studies conducted with ED participants in chronological order

Authors	Study design	Study samples	Age mean (sd)	BMI mean (sd)	Neuro-psychological Tests employed	Statistically significant performance differences (ED vs C) / study outcome	Performance at follow up
Fox, 1981	Cross-sectional Case/ mixed psychiatric clinical control	AN n=15 (1 male) PC n=15	AN 19.5 PC 21.2	Not reported	WAIS / WISC-R TMT, BVRT, WRAT	AN ↓ WAIS information and arithmetic ability. Poor performance in TMT – B and BVRT in both groups (set shift deficit not specific to AN).	NA
Hamsher, Halmi & Benton, 1981	Follow-up Pre/post treatment (1 year after hospital discharge)	AN n=20	AN 20.7 (7.7)	Baseline weight 15% below normal for age and height.	WAIS, WISC, Shipley-Hartford scale, serial digit learning, BVRT, LOT, Facial recognition, 3D constructional praxis, COWA, RT tasks.	Conducted pre-treatment 70% show at least one cognitive impairment Retarded complex reaction times associated with poor outcome	AN n=17 60% show at least one cognitive impairment = attention/concentration ↑ visuospatial processing
Small, Madero, Teagno & Ebert, 1983	Within-group No psychotropic meds.	AN n=27	AN 20.9 (5.34)	Body weight AN 32.66 kg (4.95 kg)	WAIS Rorschach	Arithmetic and Digit Span subtests from Wechsler test had better predictive value than Rorschach test in predicting percentage weight gain.	NA
Kohlmeyer, Lehmkuhl & Poutska,	Follow-up Follow up	AN n=23 (1 male)	AN 15.2 (2.1)	Body weight AN 36.5 kg	Tests of concentration, RT, IQ &		AN n=11 = IQ

1983	4 weeks after normal body weight achieved			(6.2 kg)	Perceptual speed.		↑ concentration, RT, perceptual speed.
Witt, Ryan & Hsu, 1985	Cross-sectional Case/psychiatric controls/clinical controls/ healthy controls No psychotropic meds.	AN n=16 Depression (DP) n=16 Diabetes (DB) n=16 HC n=16	AN 16.4 (1.9) DP 15.8 (1.2) DB 16.1 (1.8) HC 16.2 (2.0)	AN loss of 25% loss original body weight.	SDMT, WMS WAIS/WISC TMT	AN ↓ symbol digit paired associate test. Longer duration of illness associated with poorer SDMT performance.	NA
Kowalski, 1986	Cross sectional AN/Healthy controls/ prepubertal controls (PPC)	AN n=19 HC n=19 PPC n=19	AN 18 BN 18 PPC 11	Body weight AN 84 -125 lbs HC ? PPC ?	Proverbs Test Natural Experiments (farmer problem, baseball problem)	= problem solving /reasoning ability	NA
McKay, Humphries, Allen & Clawson, 1986	Cross-sectional No psychotropic meds for at least 2 weeks prior to study.	BN n=30 (2 male) HC n=30 (2 male)	BN 20.2 (5.0) HC 21.5 (7.7)	BN 25% under – 25% over ideal body weight HC Not reported	LNNB	BN ↓ motor (drawing speed), pathognomonic and right frontal scales.	NA

Table 2. Neuropsychological studies conducted with ED participants in chronological order (Continued)

Authors	Study design	Study samples	Age mean (sd)	BMI mean (sd)	Neuro-psychological Tests employed	Statistically significant performance differences (ED vs C) / study outcome	Performance at follow up
Strupp, Weingartner, Kaye & Gwirtsman, 1986	Cross-sectional	AN n=17 (6 weight recovered) HC n=>15 (different gps used)	AN 25.7 HC ?	Not reported	Effortful tasks: prompted recall task, paired associate test, continuous recognition task, recall task. Automatic processing tasks adapted from above	AN =/↑ effortful processing tasks AN ↓ automatic processing tasks.	NA
Touyz, Beumont & Johnstone, 1986	Cross-sectional	AN n=20 (1 male) BN n=15	AN 20.9 BN 20.2	AN 15.5 BN 20.7	WAIS/WISC, WRAT, TMT, BVRT	AN = BN No cognitive deficits found compared to theoretical norms	NA
Toner, Garfinkel & Garner, 1987	Cross sectional Participant groups determined by retrospective diagnoses	BAN n=21 RAN n=23 HC n=24 Number of above participants with partial weight restoration	BAN 28.6 (4.0) RAN 27.4 (5.3) HC 27.2 (5.3)	Body weight (% average Canadian weight for age, sex and height) BAN 82.2% RAN 84% HC 89%	MFFT	BAN participants are more cognitively impulsive than RAN participants and HC group.	NA

		(80%+) BAN n=12 RAN n=17					
Dura & Bornstein, 1989	Within subjects	AN n=20	AN 14.7 (1.78)	Not reported	WISC-R/WAIS-R WRAT	School achievement significantly greater than would be suggested by IQ test	NA
Laessle, Krieg, Fichter & Pirke, 1989	Cross sectional ED= AN + BN No psychotropic meds 4 weeks prior to study	AN n=17 BN n=22 ED n=39 HC n=22	AN 22.6 (3.8) BN 25.2 (4.9) ED 24.1 (4.6) HC 25.0 (4.8)	AN 14.0 (1.9) BN 19.8 (2.0) ED 17.2 (3.5) HC 20.3 (1.9)	CPT	AN = BN. ED group ↓ vigilance. Impaired performance is not related to cerebral atrophy.	NA
Beatty, Wonderlich, Staton & Ternes, 1990	Cross sectional Case/psychiatric control/healthy control No psychotropic meds	BN n=32 PC n=14 Depression HC n=42	BN 21.9 (5.2) PC 29.2 (7.1) HC 24.6 (7.6)	Not reported	SDMT, VF letters & categories, DF, BPSTM, Free recall and recognition.	BN & PC ↓anterograde learning, recall of verbal material and category fluency (strategy use). BN only make more rule violations in DF.	NA
Laessle, Bossert, Hank, Harlweg & Pirke, 1990	Cross sectional No psychotropic meds	BN n=30 (15 with history of AN) HC n=23	BN 24.9 (4.0) HC 25.0 (4.8)	BN 19.6 (2.4) HC 20.3 (1.9)	CPT	BN ↓vigilance Trend for performance difference between BN participants with and without history of AN	NA

Table 2. Neuropsychological studies conducted with ED participants in chronological order (Continued)

Authors	Study design	Study samples	Age mean (sd)	BMI mean (sd)	Neuro-psychological Tests employed	Statistically significant performance differences (ED vs C) / study outcome	Performance at follow up
Palazidou, Robinson & Lishman, 1990	Cross sectional	AN n=17 HC n=9	AN 25.6 (8.12) HC 29 (10.11)	% standard body weight for age and height AN 63% HC ?	BMAPS BMCST	AN = HC in test performance (mean scores) More AN score below 85% cut off in tests. Poor SDMT associated with larger cerebro-spinal fluid spaces.	NA
Jones, Duncan, Brouwers & Mirsky, 1991	Cross sectional Acute underweight AN/ Normal weight BN/ Weight restored AN (WRAN)/ Healthy controls No psychotropic meds for at least 4 weeks prior to study.	AN n=30 BN n=38 WRAN n=20 HC n=39	AN 24.4 (5.3) BN 24.1 (4.0) WRAN 26.0 (6.2) HC 24.9 (4.4)	% ideal body weight* AN 59.4 (6.6) BN 94.0 (7.3) WRAN 87.8 (11.2) HC 98.2 (7.5)	TMT, Stroop, TLCT, WCST, Category test, WAIS-R, COWAT, SAT, WMS, BSRT, RAVLT, Story recall, RFT, ROT, Purdue Pegboard, Vision test, TST, CPT, Embedded figures, RSPM	AN & BN ↓ attention focusing/execution. AN ↓ verbal, memory and visuospatial tasks. WRAN = HC.	NA
Laessle, Fischter,	Cross sectional	AN n=9 BN n=8	AN 23.8 (3.8)	AN 13.8 (1.9)	CPT	ED show poor vigilance performance:	NA

Pirke & Krieg, 1992	ED= AN + BN No psychotropic meds 4 weeks prior to study	ED n=17 HC n=22	BN 25.0 (4.4) ED 24.4 (4.0) HC 25.0 (4.8)	BN 18.9 (1.3) ED 16.4 (1.6) HC 20.3 (1.9)		Lower hit rate and perceptual sensitivity Greater impairment associated with high cortisol levels.	
Ranseen & Humphries, 1992	Cross sectional	AN n=38 BN n=54	AN 21.6 (10.01) BN 22.0 (7.04)	Not reported	WISC-R, WAIS-R	AN = BN intellectual function in line with general population. Verbal and visuospatial abilities similar.	NA
Szmukler, Andrewes, Kingston & Chen, 1992	Combined Cross sectional and follow up AN follow up prior to discharge (mean 69.8 days later) HC retested (mean 108.4 days later) No psychotropic meds	AN n=21 HC n=18	Not given but groups matched on this variable	AN 14.7 (1.9) HC ? Post treatment AN 17.7 HC ?	NART TMT, WAIS (block design only), RAVLT, SDLT, Austin Maze,	AN ↓ attention, visuospatial processing and problem solving (TMT-A,B, block design, Austin Maze) More AN participants with deficit scores	AN n= 18 HC n=18 AN = HC AN↑ Visuospatial processing, problem solving, attention-perceptual-motor functions. More AN participants with deficit scores

Table 2. Neuropsychological studies conducted with ED participants in chronological order (Continued)

Authors	Study design	Study samples	Age mean (sd)	BMI mean (sd)	Neuro-psychological Tests employed	Statistically significant performance differences (ED vs C) / study outcome	Performance at follow up
Bowers, 1994	Cross sectional	AN n=40 BN n=30	Not given	Not reported	WAIS-R, Category Test (CT), Canter Interference Procedure for the Bender Gestalt (BIP)	More AN participants show impairment in at least one test than BN. More AN impaired on BIP and CT than BN. AN show right sided deficits (BIP) and trend for difficulty shifting abstract concepts (CT).	NA
Gillberg, Rastam & Gillberg, 1994	Combined Cross sectional and follow up Follow up of AN and HC at mean age of 21 (4 years).	AN n=51 HC n=51	Baseline AN 16.1 HC 16.0 Follow up AN 21.0 HC 20.8	Baseline AN 18.3 (2.9) HC 20.2 (1.9) Follow up AN 21.2 (3.5) HC 21.2 (2.3)	Motor ability from WAIS, Dysdiadochokinesis, Hellgren speech and language assessment, eye tracking task	Dysdiadochokinesis in AN	AN n=51 HC n=51 = Dysdiadochokinesis in AN
Kaye, Bastiani & Moss, 1995	Cross sectional	AN n=9 BN n=7	AN 22 (11) BN 19 (2)	% average body weight AN=73.2% (7.6%) BN=104.5% (7.8%)	MFFT	BN responded faster than AN demonstrating impulsive cognitive style	NA

Gillberg, Gillberg, Rastam & Johansson, 1996	Case control Participants followed up over 4 years from 1992 study up.	WRAN n=51 HC n=51	WRAN 21.0 HC 20.8	WRAN 21.2 (3.5) HC 21.2 (2.3)	WAIS-R	WRAN = HC IQ identical to population norms WRAN ↓ object assembly subtest. WRAN group with autism-spectrum conditions ↓ picture arrangement .	NA
Green, Elliman, Wakeling & Rogers, 1996	Combined Cross sectional and follow up Follow up period of 12 weeks	AN n=12 HC n=17	AN 26 HC 21	Baseline AN 15.0 (0.71) HC 21.8 (21.82) Follow up AN 16.5 (0.65) HC 21.8 (0.52)	BVT, SRT, FAT, Two finger tapping, Immediate free recall	AN performed poorly in all tasks. AN ↓ free recall, SRT and motor speed.	AN n=12 HC n=17 AN = attention, free recall, motor speed, reaction time. AN did not improve cognitive performance with weight gain.
Kingston, Szmuckler, Andrews, Tress & Desmond, 1996	Combined Cross sectional and follow up Follow up AN 136.6 days (mean) HC 128.0 days (mean) 15 AN taking psychotropic meds	AN n=46 HC n=41	AN 22.1 (6.7) HC 22.0 (5.8)	Baseline AN 14.7 (1.7) HC 22.1 (1.9) Follow up / post treatment AN 17.9 (1.7)	NART, WAIS, TMT, Stroop, ROCF, Austin Maze, Memory tasks, SDLT, Supraspan	AN ↓ attention, flexibility (trend), visuospatial and memory tasks. Group deficit (%) AN > HC in attention, flexibility, visuospatial, and learning domains.	AN n=36 HC n=41 AN ↑ attention-concentration. AN = visuospatial, memory, flexibility, learning. Group deficit (%) AN > HC in learning domain.

Table 2. Neuropsychological studies conducted with ED participants in chronological order (Continued)

Authors	Study design	Study samples	Age mean (sd)	BMI mean (sd)	Neuro-psychological Tests employed	Statistically significant performance differences (ED vs C) / study outcome	Performance at follow up
Blanz, Detzner, Lay, Rose & Schmidt, 1997	Cross sectional Case/mixed psychiatric controls	AN n=160 BN n=30 PC (mixed) n=95	ED 15.4 (1.95) PC 15.4 (1.95)	Not reported	Standard German intelligence test	AN & BN ↑ PC ↓ IQ Nonverbal >verbal IQ in BN and PC groups Nonverbal =verbal IQ in AN	NA
Bradley, Taylor, Rovet, Goldberg, Hood, Wachsmuth, Azcue, & Pencharz (1997)	Combined Cross sectional and follow up	AN n=20 HC n=20	AN 15.7 (1.35) HC 15.7 (1.20)	Baseline AN 15.7 (1.20) HC 21.2 (2.65) Follow up AN 19.3 (2.43) HC 21.2 (1.52)	WISC, Visual Search Test, Mental Rotation Task, Judgment of line orientation, Card rotations test, Perceptual closure task, Coding F's task, DSPALT, Verbal and Non Verbal Memory Scale, CPT, Dichotomous listening task, Dot enumeration task.	AN = HC in all test performances.	Follow up AN n=12 (achieved 10% gain in average weight for height) HC n=11 Global improvement in performance for both groups. AN↑ HC↓ on card rotation (visuospatial) and coding F's (attention) task.
Ferraro, Wonderlich & Jocic, 1997	Cross sectional	BN n=23 HC n=28	BN & HC age range = 18-41	Not reported	SDMT, Free recall, WCST, Eckman Faces	BN trade speed for accuracy, show poorer inhibition of irrelevant information and deficiency in initiation of problem solving strategy.	NA

						BN show more variable performance in WCST and SDMT.	
Mathias & Kent, 1998	Cross sectional	AN n=34 HC n=31	AN 22 (7.4) HC 20.8 (3.6)	AN 15.3 (1.7) HC 22.8 (2.4)	NART-R,WAIS-R WMS, RAVLT, Austin Maze, ROCF, TMT, COWA	AN ↓ ability to store and retrieve logically related verbal stimuli. AN ↓ ability to recall visuospatial information after delay.	NA
Pallanti, Quercioli, Zaccara, Ramacciotti, & Ametoli, 1998	Cross sectional No psychotropic meds 8 weeks prior to study	WRAN n=28 HC n=28	WRAN 23.9 (3.4) HC 24.4 (3.8)	AN 17 pts weighed less than appropriate body weight (between 80-99%) HC ?	Electro-oculography to investigate smooth pursuit eye-movement and saccadic performance.	Eye movement abnormalities found in WRAN (a sensitive technique for examining sensory motor integration mechanisms).	NA
Lauer, Gorzewski, Gerlinghoff, Backmund & Zihl, 1999	Clinical follow up No control group Follow up post treatment (7mths after initial test period).	AN n=12 BN n=14	AN 19.7 (2.9) BN 21.9 (3.1)	% IBW Baseline AN 70.1% (7.8%) BN 99.6% (11.5%) Follow up AN 86.8% (6.8%) BN 95.8% (6.3%)	LCT, TMT, DAT, Free paragraph recall task, CVLT, Corsi span, RSPM, DLPST	AN = BN in all tests. AN and BN show anomalous performance in attention and problem solving tasks.	AN n=12 BN n=14 AN = BN ↑ TMT, DAT, LCT, RSPM. Impairment reduces with clinical remission. Performance measures are not related to clinical outcome.

Table 2. Neuropsychological studies conducted with ED participants in chronological order (Continued)

Authors	Study design	Study samples	Age mean (sd)	BMI mean (sd)	Neuro-psychological Tests employed	Statistically significant performance differences (ED vs C) / study outcome	Performance at follow up
Seed, Dixon, McCluskey & Young, 2000	Cross sectional	AN n=18 HC n=18	AN 27.3 HC age matched	AN 15.2 (2.05) HC 22.3 (1.65)	Computer based Vigilance task, CANTAB, AVLT	AN ↓ attention (vigilance) and memory (delayed recall). No association found between performance and cortisol levels.	NA
Neumarker, Bzufka, Dudeck, Hein & Neumarker, 2000	Combined Cross sectional and follow up AN retested upon restoration of normal body weight (mean 132 days).	AN n=18 HC n=25	AN 14.4 (1.59) HC 15.8 (1.57)	AN 14.9 (1.36) HC 20.5 (2.3) Follow up AN 18.95	General Fluid Ability and General Crystallized Ability, Vocabulary battery and Number sequences	AN ↓ number processing and fluid intelligence when underweight.	AN n=18 AN ↑ numeric skills and fluid intelligence Prevalence of impaired arithmetic performance in line with population norms.
Tchanturia, Serpell, Troop & Treasure, 2001	Cross-sectional	AN n=15 BN n=15 HC n=28	AN 28.1 (7.3) BN 25.1 (7.1) HC 28.2 (5.6)	AN 14.1 (2.2) BN 20.0 (2.3) HC 22.3 (2.1)	Haptic Illusion Task	AN & BN ↑ perceptual errors but show different response styles. AN↑ perceptual rigidity as measured by perseverations. BN ↑ unstable, fluctuating responses.	NA

Grunwald, Ettrich, Assmann, Daehne, & Krause, 2001	Combined Cross sectional and follow up AN follow up 1 month after hospital discharge (mean 449 days).	AN n=10 HC n=10	AN 15.9 (1.97) HC 16.1 (0.74)	AN 15.2 (1.27) HC 22.2 (3.01) Follow up AN 16.6 (1.71)	Haptic exploration Task	AN ↓ reproduction of the haptic material	AN n=10 = processing haptic material Poor somatosensory integration processing regardless of the stage of illness.
Bayless, Kanz, Moser, McDowell, Bowers, Andersen & Paulsen, 2002	Cases only	AN n=59	AN 24.3 (8.0)	AN 16.8 (2.4)	WAIS III, WMT III, BVRT, COWA, TMT, WRAT	Half of the patients had mild cognitive impairment on two or more tasks ($\leq 9^{th}$ percentile) 1/3 failed in 2 or more tasks ($\leq 5^{th}$ percentile) Memory appears particularly affected	NA
Fassino, Piero, Daga, Leombruni, Mortara & Rovera, 2002	Cross sectional	AN n=20 HC n=20	AN 23.3 (6.6) HC 23.1 (2.9)	AN 15.6 (2.2) HC 20.6 (1.7)	Modified Stroop (ED related stimuli and control words), WCST	AN ↓ abstraction ability and flexibility of thought in WCST AN ↓ modified stroop (non-specific attention bias)	NA
Grunwald, Ettrich, Busse, Assmann, Dahne, Gertz. 2002	Cross sectional	AN n=16 HC n=16	AN 15.3 (1.79) HC 16.3 (1.04)	AN 14.8 (1.05) HC 19.2 (1.67)	Angle adjustment without visual feedback	AN ↓ performance on right sided haptic task	NA

Table 2. Neuropsychological studies conducted with ED participants in chronological order (Continued)

Authors	Study design	Study samples	Age mean (sd)	BMI mean (sd)	Neuro-psychological Tests employed	Statistically significant performance differences (ED vs C) / study outcome	Performance at follow up
Murphy, Nutzinger, Paul & Leplow, 2002	Cross sectional 2x AN, 4x BN on psychotropic meds.	AN n=16 BN n=16 HC n=16	AN 22.3 (4.4) BN 22.0 (4.5) HC 25.3 (2.6)	AN 14.8 (1.2) BN 20.1 (2.3) HC 22.0 (2.6)	WAIS, BSRT, COWA, ROCF, SDMT, TMT, CAL (neutral and ED threatening words)	AN ↓ BN & HC↑ CAL with neutral stimuli. AN=BN=HC CAL with ED stimuli AN=BN=HC in other neuropsychological performance measures.	NA
Seed, McCue, Wesnes, Dahabra & Young ,2002	Cross sectional	AN n=25 HC n=20	AN 29.1 (1.88) HC 29.3 (1.91)	AN 14.2 (0.46) HC 22.4 (0.70)	CDR computerised assessment system	AN ↓ simple RT & choice RT, digit vigilance, immediate word recall, word and picture recognition, memory scanning. No relationship between cortisol measures and cognitive performance.	NA
Tchanturia, Morris, Surguladze & Treasure, 2002	Cross sectional No psychotropic meds.	AN n=30 RecAN n=16 HC n=23	AN 25 (6.7) RecAN 30 (6.0) HC 27.6 (6.4)	AN 14.6 (2.1) RecAN 20.1 (1.7) HC 21.3 (1.8)	COWA, Haptic Illusion Task (perceptual shifting), CATBAT (cognitive shifting).	AN = RecAN AN, RecAN ↓ HC↑ cognitive and perceptual flexibility in set shifting tasks	NA
Dodin & Nandrino	Cross sectional	AN n=12 HC n=11	AN 23.2 (5.5)	AN 15.4 HC 21.04	Simple and complex body	Behavioural results: AN↑ complex BI recognition.	NA

2003			HC 22.8 (3.2)		image discrimination. Simple and complex geometrical shape discrimination.	Physiological results: AN ERPs shows non-specific hyperarousal.	
Galderisi, Mucci, Monteleone, Sorrentino, Piegari & Maj, 2003	Cross sectional ED = AN + BN No psychotropic meds (3 pts with 6 week wash out period)	AN n=14 BN n=31 HC n=45	ED 23.7 (4.54) HC 24.22 (4.8)	AN 15.3 (2.23) BN 21.5 (2.30) HC ?	WAIS-R, SCAL, NSCAL, SOPT, HDRS, Corsi bock tapping, self ordered pointing task, block span, digit span.	AN = BN. ED slower on incidental learning task ED more accurate in executive task guided by external feedback.	NA
Lawrence, Dowson, Foxall, Summerfield , Robbins & Sahakian, 2003	Cross sectional	AN n=12 HC n=12	AN 25.7 (7.2) HC 26.7 (6.2)	AN 15.8 (1.4) HC 24.4 (4.0)	Visual discrimination learning, Pattern recognition.	↓ visual discrimination lerning	NA
McDowell, Bradley, Moser, Ferneyhough , Bowers, Andersen, & Paulsen, 2003	Cases only	AN n=98 (9 male)	AN 27.0 (8.05) (range 15-50)	AN 15.8 (2.69) (range 9-24)	WAIS-R	No relation between cognitive abilities and depression in AN.	NA

Table 2. Neuropsychological studies conducted with ED participants in chronological order (Continued)

Authors	Study design	Study samples	Age mean (sd)	BMI mean (sd)	Neuro-psychological Tests employed	Statistically significant performance differences (ED vs C) / study outcome	Performance at follow up
Moser, Benjamin, Bayless, McDowell, Paulsen, Bowers, Arndt, Andersen, 2003	Follow up Baseline test on admission to hospital inpatient programme, follow up at discharge (mean 32.79 days).	AN n=28	AN 26.4 (8.70)	Baseline AN 16.5 (2.49) Follow up/post treatment AN 19.2 (1.49)	Repeatable Battery for the Assessment of Neuropsychological Status	Overall mean neuropsychological performance at admission was at lower limit of average range.	AN n=28 ↑ Total test battery scale score domain score analyses show: ↑ psychomotor speed and memory
Pieters, Sabbe, Hulstijn, Probst, Vandereyken & Peuskens, 2003	Cross sectional	AN n=32 HC n=32	AN 18.0 (2.6) HC 17.7 (2.1)	AN 14.4 (1.4) HC 21.2 (1.5)	Psychomotor tasks : drawing + copying	AN show cognitive style of speed over accuracy: AN faster in drawing task. AN reaction times shorter in copy task, with more errors.	NA
Murphy, Nutzinger, Paul & Leplow, 2004	Cross sectional ED/psychiatric controls (OCD)/ Healthy controls 2x AN, 4x BN on	AN n=16 BN n=16 OCD n=16 HC n=16	AN 22.3 (4.4) BN 22.0 (4.5) OCD 25.1 (5.4) HC 25.3 (2.6)	AN 14.8 (1.2) BN 20.1 (2.3) OCD 22.9 (3.5) HC 22.0 (2.6)	WAIS, BSRT, COWA letter, category and alternation, SDMT, ROCF, TMT, CAL – neutral and threatening/emotional (disorder	OCD & AN ↓ BN & HC ↑ CAL with emotionally neutral stimuli All groups equal on CAL with disease specific stimuli. OCD ↓ mental flexibility, visual search and attention vs AN, BN, HC.	NA

	psychotropic meds				specific).	BN ↑ visual memory vs AN.	
Ohrmann, Kersting, Suslow, Lalee-Mentzel, Donges, Fiebich, Arolt, Heindel & Pfleiderer, 2004.	Cross sectional No psychotropic meds	AN n=11 HC n=11	AN 22.7 (3.8) HC 27.5 (6.3)	AN 15.2 (1.22) HC 21.3 (2.80)	WAIS-R, AVLT, visual learning and memory, WCST, Divided attention, Go-No-Go	AN showed poorer performance in all tests. AN ↓ WAIS (vocab), verbal learning and divided attention task. Cognitive impairments correlated with neuronal and glial cell pathology of the frontal cortex.	NA
Tchanturia, Anderluh, Morris, Rabe-Hesketh, Collier, Sanchez & Treasure, 2004a	Cross sectional	AN n=34 BN n=19 HC n=35	AN 26.7 (7.9) BN 26.5 (5.7) HC 24.8 (4.7)	AN 13.7 (1.4) BN 21.8 (2.1) HC 21.8 (1.7)	COWA, TMT, Brixton test, CATBAT (cognitive set shifting), Haptic Illusions (perceptual set shifting), Picture set test, Dysdiadodokinesis	AN & BN ↓ mental flexibility Different neuropsychological profiles in set shifting tasks seen across disorders (AN & BN).	NA

Table 2. Neuropsychological studies conducted with ED participants in chronological order (Continued)

Authors	Study design	Study samples	Age mean (sd)	BMI mean (sd)	Neuro-psychological Tests employed	Statistically significant performance differences (ED vs C) / study outcome	Performance at follow up
Tchanturia, Morris, Brecelj, Anderluh, Nikolaou & Treasure, 2004b	Combined cross sectional and follow up Baseline test upon admission to inpatient treatment. Follow up upon weight gain (BMI > 17.5, ANWR).	AN n= 34 ANRec n=18 HC n=36	AN 27.2 (8.3) ANRec 28.4 (6.8) HC 24.9 (4.8)	AN 13.7 (1.4) ANRec 20.4 (1.5) HC 21.8 (1.7) Follow up ANWR 18.4 (1.4)	COWA, TMT, Brixton test, CATBAT (cognitive set shifting), Haptic Illusions (perceptual set shifting), Picture Set test,	Performance impairment in shifting tasks: AN > RecAN > HC AN ↓ HC ↑ TMT, Brixton, Picture set. AN ↓ HC & RecAN ↑ perceptual and cognitive shifting.	AN n= 22 = Brixton, TMT, perceptual set shifting. ↑ speed of cognitive set shifting
Holliday, Tchanturia, Landau, Collier & Treasure, in review	Cross sectional Sister pair design and non related controls	AN n=47 (RecAN n=23) SIS n=47 HC n=47	AN 26.3 (10.2) SIS 27.6 (9.6) HC 26.5 (6.1)	AN 17.9 (2.7) SIS 22.8 (4.4) HC 21.1 (2.3)	COWA, TMT, Brixton test, CATBAT (cognitive set shifting), Haptic Illusions (perceptual set shifting), Picture Set test, Dysdiadodokinesis	AN & SIS ↓ HC ↑ set shifting AN = SIS set shifting measures. AN = RecAN set shifting measures. Sisters discordant for AN performed similarly to AN in perceptual and cognitive shift tasks	NA

AN = Anorexia Nervosa, BN = Bulimia Nervosa, RAN = AN restricting subtype, BAN = AN bulimic subtype, WRAN = Weight restored AN, RecAN = Recovered AN, ANSis = Healthy sister of AN proband (discordant for AN), HC = Healthy control, PC = Psychiatric control

IBW* % ideal body weight according to the Metropolitan Life Insurance company tables. Psychotropic meds = Psychotropic medication. ? = Data not reported

Performance symbols: = equal performance, no difference between groups; ↑ higher performance than other groups; ↓ poorer performance than other groups.

Follow up symbols: = no improvement in performance compared to baseline, ↑ improvement in performance compared to baseline

REQUIREMENTS AND RECOMMENDATIONS FOR FUTURE RESEARCH

Future research requires careful design in order to try and address the many complex issues highlighted here. Longitudinal studies are needed, following participants into recovery, not just based on weight gain but on major symptom remission. To address the question of sub-types and cognitive functioning being related to specific psychopathology, ED participant groups should be kept as homogeneous in symptom profile as possible according to the current categorical approach to diagnosis. Alternatively neuropsychological functioning could be analysed according to symptom dimensions, in line with the contemporary literature highlighting underlying similarities rather than differences across diagnostic categories (Fairburn and Harrison, 2003). As well as carefully matched healthy control groups, psychiatric controls should be incorporated into future research to investigate the specificity of dysfunction, especially involving disorders thought to be similar in phenomenology and frequently found to be comorbid with EDs, such as OCD and major depression respectively. It is of great importance that the underlying cognitive constructs of the tests utilised are clearly defined and uniformly applied across studies, enabling the development of reliable conclusions with the potential for replication.

We endorse the use of a hypothesis driven approach to neuropsychological investigations, avoiding the use of large multidimensional test batteries which limit statistical power and have limited scope for theoretical advances. In accordance, our current research is widening the exploration of potential neuropsychological traits, targeting cognitive skills associated with potential anatomical areas of dysfunction as highlighted in neuroimaging studies and information processes which parallel the personality and behavioural traits associated with EDs. Such neuropsychological domains include response inhibition, decision making and extinction processing.

The identification of biological phenotypes and thus potential endophenotypes of EDs, has major theoretical and clinical implications. Such knowledge will aid the search for susceptibility genes significantly and enhance our understanding of the biological mechanisms through which they work. Furthermore, uncovering the biological underpinnings of disorder and their expression through cognition, personality and behaviour, will aid the development of more appropriate and specialised treatment strategies for those who suffer from these debilitating disorders.

REFERENCES

American Psychiatric Association (1994). *Diagnostic and statistical manual of mental disorders*. (4 ed.) Washington.

Anderluh, M. B., Tchanturia, K., Rabe-Hesketh, S., & Treasure, J. (2003). Childhood obsessive-compulsive personality traits' in adult women with eating disorders: Defining a broader eating disorder phenotype. *American Journal of Psychiatry,* 160, 242-247.

Askenazy, F., Candito, M., Caci, H., Myquel, M., Chambon, P., Darcourt, G. et al. (1998). Whole blood serotonin content, tryptophan concentrations, and impulsivity in anorexia nervosa. *Biological Psychiatry,* 43, 188-195.

Bakan, R., Birmingham, C. L., & Goldner, E. M. (1990). Chronicity in anorexia nervosa: Pregnancy and birth complications as risk factors. *International Journal of Eating Disorders,* 10, 631-645.

Bardo, M. T., Donohew, R. L., & Harrington, N. G. (1996). Psychobiology of novelty seeking behaviour. *Behavioural Brain Research,* 77, 23-43.

Barkley, R. A. (1997). Behavioural inhibition, sustained attention, and executive functions: Constructing a unifying theory of ADHD. *Psychological Bulletin,* 121, 65-94.

Bayless, J. D., Kanz, J. E., Moser, D. J., McDowell, B. D., Bowers, W. A., Andersen, A. et al. (2002). Neuropsychological characteristics of patients in a hospital-based eating disorder program. *Annals of Clinical Psychiatry,* 14, 203-207.

Beatty, W. W., Wonderlich, S. A., Staton, R. D., & Ternes, L. A. (1990). Cognitive functioning in bulimia: Comparison with depression. *Bulletin of the Psychonomic Society,* 28, 289-292.

Bechara, A., Damasio, A. R., Damasio, H., & Anderson, S. W. (1994). Insensitivity to future consequences following damage to human prefrontal cortex. *Cognition,* 50, 7-15.

Ben-Tovim, D., Walker, M. K., Fok, D., & Yap, E. (1989). An adaption of the stroop test for measuring shape and food concerns in eating disorders: A quantitative measure of psychopathology? *International Journal of Eating Disorders,* 8, 681-687.

Bezeau, S. & Graves, R. (2001). Statistical power and effect sizes of clinical neuropsychology research. *Journal of Clinical and Experimental Neuropsychology,* 23, 399-406.

Blanz, B. J., Detzner, U., Lay, B., Rose, F., & Schmidt, M. H. (1997). The intellectual functioning of adolescents with anorexia nervosa and bulimia nervosa. *European Child & Adolescent Psychiatry,* 6, 129-135.

Bowers, W. A. (1994). Neuropsychological impairment among anorexia nervosa and bulimia patients. *Eating Disorders: the Journal of Treatment & Prevention,* 2, 42-46.

Bradley, S. J., Taylor, M. J., Rovet, J. F., Goldberg, E., Hood, J., Wachsmuth, R. et al. (1997). Assessment of brain function in adolescent anorexia nervosa before and after weight gain. *Journal of Clinical & Experimental Neuropsychology,* 19, 20-33.

Braun, C. M. J. & Chouinard, M. J. (1992). Is Anorexia-Nervosa A Neuropsychological Disease. *Neuropsychology Review,* 3, 171-212.

Brewerton, T. D. (1995). Toward a unified theory of serotonin dysregulation in eating and related disorders. *Psychoneuroendocrinology,* 20, 561-590.

Briskman, J., Happe, F., & Frith, U. (2001). Exploring the cognitive phenotype of autism: Weak 'central coherence' in parents and siblings of children with autism: 2. Real-life skills and preferences. *Journal of Child Psychology & Psychiatry & Allied Disciplines,* 42, 309-316.

Bulik, C. M., Tozzi, F., Anderson, C., Mazzeo, S. E., Aggen, S., & Sullivan, P. F. (2003). The relation between eating disorders and components of perfectionism. *American Journal of Psychiatry,* 160, 366-368.

Burgess, P. W. (1997). Theory and methodology in executive function research. In P.Rabbitt (Ed.), *Methodology of frontal and executive function* (pp. 81-116). East Sussex: Psychology Press.

Cannon, C. M. & Bseikri, M. R. (2004). Is dopamine required for natural reward? *Physiology & Behavior,* 81, 741-748.

Casper, R. (1990). Personality features of women with good outcome from restricting anorexia nervosa. *Psychosomatic Medicine,* 52, 156-170.

Cavedini, P., Bassi, T., Ubbiali, A., Casolari, A., Giordani, S., Zorzi, C. et al. (2004). Neuropsychological investigation of decision-making in anorexia nervosa. *Psychiatry Research, 127,* 259-266.

Claes, L., Vandereycken, W., & Vertommen, H. (2002). Impulsive and compulsive traits in eating disordered patients compared with controls. *Personality & Individual Differences, 32,* 707-714.

Cnattingius, S., Hultman, C. M., Dahl, M., & Sparen, P. (1999). Very preterm birth, birth trauma, and the risk of anorexia nervosa among girls. *Archives of General Psychiatry, 56,* 634-638.

Connan, F., Campbell, I. C., Katzman, M., Lightman, S. L., & Treasure, J. (2003). A neurodevelopmental model for anorexia nervosa. *Physiology & Behavior., 79,* 13-24.

Cools, R., Barker, R. A., Sahakian, B. J., & Robbins, T. W. (2003). L-Dopa medication remediates cognitive inflexibility, but increases impulsivity in patients with Parkinson's disease. *Neuropsychologia, 41,* 1431-1441.

Cooper, M. & Todd, G. (1997). Selective processing of three types of stimuli in eating disorders. *British Journal of Clinical Psychology., 36,* 279-281.

Cuesta, M. J., Peralta, V., & Zarzuela, A. (2001). Are personality traits associated with cognitive disturbance in psychosis. *Schizophrenia Research, 51,* 109-117.

Cummings, J. L. (1993). Frontal-subcortical circuits and human behaviour. *Archives of Neurology, 50,* 873-880.

DaCosta, M. & Halmi, K. A. (1992). Classifications of anorexia nervosa: Question of subtypes. *International Journal of Eating Disorders, 11,* 305-313.

Davies, H. & Tchanturia, K. (2005). Cognitive remediation therapy: A case study with a patient with anorexia nervosa. *European Eating Disorders Review, In press.*

Delvenne, V., Goldman, S., De, M. V., & Lostra, F. (1999). Brain glucose metabolism in eating disorders assessed by positron emission tomography. *International Journal of Eating Disorders, 25,* 29-37.

Dobson, K. S. & Dozois, D. J. A. (2004). Attentional biases in eating disorders: A meta-analytic review of Stroop performance. *Clinical Psychology Review, 23,* 1001-1022.

Dodin, V. & Nandrino, J. L. (2003). Cognitive processing of anorexic patients in recognition tasks: An event-related potentials study. *International Journal of Eating Disorders, 33,* 299-307.

Dura, J. R. & Bornstein, R. A. (1989). Differences between IQ and school achievement in anorexia nervosa. *Journal of Clinical Psychology,* 45, 433-435.

Eddy, K. T., Keel, P. K., Dorer, D. J., Delinsky, S. S., Franko, D. L., & Herzog, D. B. (2002). Longitudinal comparison of anorexia nervosa subtypes. *Int J Eat Disord.,* 31, 191-201.

Eslinger, P. J. & Grattan, L. M. (1993). Frontal lobe and frontal-striatal substrates for different forms of human cognitive flexibility. *Neuropsychologia,* 31, 17-28.

Eysenck, H. J. (1947). *Dimensions of Personality*. Oxford: K. Paul, Trench, Trubner.

Fahy, T. & Eisler, I. (1993). Impulsivity and eating disorders. *British Journal of Psychiatry,* 162, 193-197.

Fairburn, C. G. & Harrison, P. J. (2003). Eating disorders. *Lancet,* 361, 407-416.

Fairburn, C. G., Cooper, Z., & Shafran, R. (2003). Cognitive behaviour therapy for eating disorders: A "transdiagnostic" theory and treatment. *Behaviour Research & Therapy,* 41, 509-528.

Fassino, S., Piero, A., Daga, G. A., Leombruni, P., Mortara, P., & Rovera, G. G. (2002). Attentional biases and frontal functioning in anorexia nervosa. *International Journal of Eating Disorders,* 31, 274-283.

Ferraro, F. R., Wonderlich, S., & Jocic, Z. (1997). Performance variability as a new theoretical mechanism regarding eating disorders and cognitive processing. *Journal of Clinical Psychology.,* 53, 117-121.

Fessler, D. M. T. (2002). Pseudoparadoxical impulsivity in restrictive anorexia nervosa: A consequence of the logic of scarcity. *International Journal of Eating Disorders,* 31, 376-388.

Foley, D. L., Thacker, L. R., Aggen, S. H., Neale, M. C., & Kendler, K. S. (2001). Pregnancy and perinatal complications associated with risks for common psychiatric disorders in a population-based sample of female twins. *Am.J Med Genet.,* 105, 426-431.

Fox, C. F. (1981). Neuropsychological correlates of anorexia nervosa. *International Journal of Psychiatry in Medicine,* 11, 285-290.

Frank, G. K., Kaye, W. H., Weltzin, T. E., Perel, J., Moss, H., McConaha, C. et al. (2001). Altered response to meta-chlorophenylpiperazine in anorexia nervosa: Support for a persistent alteration of serotonin activity after short-term weight restoration. *International Journal of Eating Disorders,* 30, 57-68.

Galderisi, S., Mucci, A., Monteleone, P., Sorrentino, D., Piegari, G., & Maj, M. (2003). Neurocognitive functioning in subjects with eating disorders: The influence of neuroactive steroids. *Biological Psychiatry, 53,* 921-927.

Gillberg, C., Rastam, M., & Gillberg, I. C. (1994). Anorexia nervosa: Physical health and neurodevelopment at 16 and 21 years. *Developmental Medicine & Child Neurology, 36,* 567-575.

Gillberg, I. C., Gillberg, C., Rastam, M., & Johansson, M. (1996). The cognitive profile of anorexia nervosa: a comparative study including a community-based sample. *Compr.Psychiatry, 37,* 23-30.

Gogtay, N., Giedd, J. N., Lusk, L., Hayashi, K. M., Greenstein, D., Vaituzis, A. C. et al. (2004). Dynamic mapping of human cortical development during childhood through early adulthood. *PNAS,* 101, 8174-8179.

Gray, J. A. & McNaughton, N. (2000). *The Neuropsychiatry of Anxiety: An enquiry into the functions of the septo-hippocampal system (2nd ed.).* New York: Oxford University Press.

Green, M. W., Elliman, N. A., Wakeling, A., & Rogers, P. J. (1996). Cognitive functioning, weight change and therapy in anorexia nervosa. *Journal of Psychiatric Research,* 30, 401-410.

Grunwald, M., Ettrich, C., Busse, F., Assmann, B., Dahne, A., & Gertz, H. J. (2002). Angle paradigm - A new method to measure right parietal dysfunctions in anorexia nervosa. *Archives of Clinical Neuropsychology,* 17, 485-496.

Grunwald, M., Ettrich, C., Assmann, B., Daehne, A., & Krause, W. (2001). Deficits in haptic perception and right parietal theta power changes in patients with anorexia nervosa before and after weight gain. *International Journal of Eating Disorders,* 29, 417-428.

Hamsher, K., Halmi, K., & Benton, A. L. (1981). Prediction of outcome in anorexia nervosa from neuropsychological status. *Psychiatry Research,* 4, 79-99.

Happe, F. (1999). Autism: cognitive deficit or cognitive style? *Trends in Cognitive Sciences,* 3, 216-222.

Happe, F., Briskman, J., & Frith, U. (2001). Exploring the cognitive phenotype of autism: Weak 'central coherence' in parents and siblings of children with autism: 1. Experimental tests. *Journal of Child Psychology & Psychiatry & Allied Disciplines,* 42, 299-307.

Heinrichs, R. W. & Zakzanis, K. K. (1998). Neurocognitive deficit in schizophrenia: a quantitative review of the evidence. *Neuropsychology.,* 12, 426-445.

Hollander, E. (1998). Treatment of obsessive-compulsive spectrum disorders with SSRIs. *British Journal of Psychiatry,* 173, 7-12.

Hollander, E. (1993). Obsessive-compulsive spectrum disorders: An overview. *Psychiatric Annals,* 23, 355-358.

Holliday, J., Tchanturia, K., Landau, S., Collier, D. A., & Treasure, J. (2005). Is impaired set shifting an endophenotype of anorexia nervosa. *American Journal of Psychiatry, In press.*

Jones, B. P., Duncan, C. C., Brouwers, P., & Mirsky, A. F. (1991). Cognition in Eating Disorders. *Journal of Clinical and Experimental Neuropsychology,* 13, 711-728.

Katzman, D. K., Christensen, B., Young, A. R., & Zipursky, R. B. (2001). Starving the brain: structural abnormalities and cognitive impairment in adolescents with anorexia nervosa. *Semin.Clin.Neuropsychiatry,* 6, 146-152.

Kaye, W. H., Bastiani, A. M., & Moss, H. (1995). Cognitive style of patients with anorexia nervosa and bulimia nervosa. *International Journal of Eating Disorders.,* 18, 287-290.

Kaye, W. H., Frank, G. K., & McConaha, C. (1999). Altered dopamine activity after recovery from restricting-type anorexia nervosa. *Neuropsychopharmacology,* 21, 503-506.

Kaye, W. H., Frank, G. K., Meltzer, C. C., Price, J. C., McConaha, C. W., Crossan, P. J. et al. (2001). Altered serotonin 2A receptor activity in women who have recovered from bulimia nervosa. *Am.J Psychiatry,* 158, 1152-1155.

Kaye, W. H., Klump, K. L., Frank, G. K. W., & Strober, M. (2000). Anorexia and bulimia nervosa. *Annual Review of Medicine,* 51, 299-313.

Kaye, W. H., Lilenfeld, L. R., Berrettini, W. H., Strober, M., Devlin, B., Klump, K. L. et al. (2000). A search for susceptibility loci for anorexia nervosa: Methods and sample description. *Biological Psychiatry,* 47, 794-803.

Keefe, R. S. E. (1995). The contribution of neuropsychology to psychiatry. *American Journal of Psychiatry,* 152, 6-15.

Kingston, K., Szmuckler, G., Andrews, D., Tress, B., & Desmond, P. (1996). Neuropsychological and structural brain changes in anorexia nervosa before and after refeeding. *Psychological Medicine,* 26, 15-28.

Kohlmeyer, K., Lehmkuhl, G., & Poutska, F. (1983). Computed tomography of anorexia nervosa. *AJNR,* 4, 437-438.

Krueger, R. F. (1999). Personality traits in late adolescence predict mental disorders in early adulthood: A prospective-epidemiological study. *Journal of Personality,* 67, 39-65.

Kuelz, A. K., Hohagen, F., & Voderholzer, U. (2004). Neuropsychological performance in obsessive-compulsive disorder: a critical review. *Biol.Psychol., 65,* 185-236.

Laessle, R. G., Bossert, S., Hank, G., Hahlweg, K., & Pirke, K. M. (1990). Cognitive performance in patients with bulimia nervosa: relationship to intermittent starvation. *Biological Psychiatry., 27,* 549-551.

Laessle, R. G., Fischer, M., Fichter, M. M., Pirke, K. M., & Krieg, J. C. (1992). Cortisol levels and vigilance in eating disorder patients. *Psychoneuroendocrinology., 17,* 475-484.

Laessle, R. G., Krieg, J. C., Fichter, M. M., & Pirke, K. M. (1989). Cerebral atrophy and vigilance performance in patients with anorexia nervosa and bulimia nervosa. *Neuropsychobiology., 21,* 187-191.

Lambe, E. K., Katzman, D. K., Mikulis, D. J., & Kennedy, S. H. (1997). Cerebral gray matter volume deficits after weight recovery from anorexia nervosa. *Archives of General Psychiatry, 54,* 537-542.

Lauer, C. J. (2002). Neuropsychological findings in eating disorders. In H.D'haenen, J.A.den Boer, & P.Willner (Eds.), *Textbook of Biological Psychiatry* (pp. 1167-1172). Chichester: John Wiley & Sons.

Lauer, C. J., Gorzewski, B., Gerlingloff, M., Backmund, H., & Zihl, J. (1999). Neuropsychological assessments before and after treatment in patients with anorexia nervosa and bulimia nervosa. *Journal of Psychiatric Research., 33,* 129-138.

Lauer, C. J., Laessle, R. G., & Fichter, M. M. (1990). Structural brain alterations and binging and vomiting behaviour in eating disorder patients. *International Journal of Eating Disorders, 9,* 161-166.

Laurent, A., Duly, D., Murry, P., Foussard, N., Boccara, S., Mingat, F. et al. (2001). WCST performance and schizotypal features in the first degree relatives of patients with schizophrenia. *Psychiatry Research, 104,* 133-144.

Lawrence, A. D., Dowson, J., Foxall, G. L., Summerfield, R., Robbins, T. W., & Sahakian, B. J. (2003). Impaired visual discrimination learning in anorexia nervosa. *Appetite, 40,* 85-89.

Lee, M. & Shafran, R. (2004). Information processing biases in eating disorders. *Clinical Psychology Review, 24,* 215-238.

Lena, S. M., Fiocco, A. J., & Leyenaar, J. K. (2004). The role of cognitive deficits in the development of eating disorders. *Neuropsychology Review, 14,* 99-113.

Lezak, (1995). *Neuropsychological Assessment.* (3 ed.) Oxford: Oxford University Press.

Lilenfeld, L. R. R., Devlin, B., Bacanu, S., Kaye, W. H., Bulik, C. M., Strober, M. et al. (2001). Deriving behavioural phenotypes in an international, multi-centre study of eating disorders. *Psychological Medicine,* 31, 635-645.

Logan, G. D., Schachar, R. J., & Tannock, R. (1997). Impulsivity and inhibitory control. *Psychological Science,* 8, 60-64.

Lou, H. C., Hansen, D., Nordentoft, M., & Pryds, O. (1994). Prenatal stressors of human life affect fetal brain development. *Developmental Medicine & Child Neurology,* 36,826-832.

Lucki, I. (1998). The spectrum of behaviors influenced by serotonin. *Biological Psychiatry,* 44, 151-162.

Lupien, S., Lecours, A. R., Lussier, I., Schwartz, G., Nair, N. P. V., & Meaney, M. J. (1994). Basal cortisol levels and cognitive deficits in human aging. *Journal of Neuroscience,* 14, 2893-2903.

Mathias, J. L. & Kent, P. S. (1998). Neuropsychological consequences of extreme weight loss and dietary restriction in patients with anorexia nervosa. *Journal of Clinical and Experimental Neuropsychology,* 20, 548-564.

McDowell, B. D., Moser, D. J., Ferneyhough, K., Bowers, W. A., Andersen, A. E., & Paulsen, J. S. (2003). Cognitive impairment in anorexia nervosa in not due to depressed mood. *International Journal of Eating Disorders,* 33, 351-355.

McKay, S. E., Humphries, L. L., Allen, M. E., & Clawson, D. R. (1986). Neuropsychological test performance of bulimic patients. *International Journal of Neuroscience,* 30, 73-80.

Mintz, L. B. & Betz, N. E. (1988). Prevalence and correlates of eating disordered behaviours among undergraduate women. *Journal of Counseling Psychology,* 35, 463-471.

Miyake, A., Friedman, N. P., Emerson, M. J., Witzki, A. H., & Howerter, A. (2000). The unity and diversity of executive functions and their contributions to complex "frontal lobe" tasks: A latent variable analysis. *Cognitive Psychology,* 41, 49-100.

Moser, D. J., Benjamin, M. L., Bayless, J. D., McDowell, B. D., Paulsen, J. S., Bowers, W. A. et al. (2003). Neuropsychological functioning pretreatment and posttreatment in an inpatient eating disorders program. *International Journal of Eating Disorders,* 33, 64-70.

Murphy, F. C., Smith, K. A., Cowen, P. J., Robbins, T. W., & Sahakian, B. J. (2002). The effects of tryptophan depletion on cognitive and affective processing in healthy volunteers. *Psychopharmacology,* 163, 42-53.

Murphy, R., Nutzinger, D. O., Paul, T., & Leplow, B. (2004). Conditional-associative learning in eating disorders: A comparison with OCD. *Journal of Clinical & Experimental Neuropsychology.*, 190-199.

Murphy, R., Nutzinger, D. O., Paul, T., & Leplow, B. (2002). Dissociated conditional-associative learning in anorexia nervosa. *Journal of Clinical & Experimental Neuropsychology, 24,* 176-186.

Naruo, T., Nakabeppu, Y., Sagiyama, K. i., Munemoto, T., Homan, N., Deguchi, D. et al. (2000). Characteristic regional cerebral blood flow patterns in anorexia nervosa patients with binge/purge behavior. *American Journal of Psychiatry, 157,* 1520-1522.

Newton, J. R., Freeman, C. P., & Munro, J. (1993). Impulsivity and dyscontrol in bulimia nervosa: is impulsivity an independent phenomenon or a marker of severity? *Acta Psychiatrica Scandinavica, 87,* 389-394.

Nozoe, S., Naruo, T., Nakabeppu, Y., Soejima, Y., Nakajo, M., & Tanaka, H. (1993). Changes in regional cerebral blood flow in patients with anorexia nervosa detected through single photon emission tomography imaging. *Biol.Psychiatry, 34,* 578-580.

Nozoe, S., Naruo, T., Yonekura, R., Nakabeppu, Y., Soejima, Y., Nagai, N. et al. (1995). Comparison of regional cerebral blood flow in patients with eating disorders. *Brain Res.Bull., 36,* 251-255.

O'Brien, K. M. & Vincent, N. K. (2003). Psychiatric comorbidity in anorexia and bulimia nervosa: nature, prevalence, and causal relationships. *Clinical Psychology Review, 23,* 57-74.

O'Connor, T. G., Heron, J., Golding, J., Beveridge, M., & Glover, V. (2002). Maternal antenatal anxiety and children's behavioural/emotional problems at four years: Report from the Avon Longitudinal Study of Parents and Children. *British Journal of Psychiatry,* 180, 502-508.

Ohrmann, P., Kersting, A., Suslow, T., Lalee-Mentzel, J., Donges, U., Fiebich, M. et al. (2004). Proton magnetic resonance specrroscopy in anorexia nervosa: correllations with cognition. *NeuroReport,* 15, 549-553.

Palazidou, E., Robinson, P., & Lishman, W. A. (1990). Neuroradiological and neuropsychological assessment in anorexia nervosa. *Psychological Medicine, 20,*
521-527.

Pallanti, S., Quercioli, L., Zaccara, G., Ramacciotti, A. B., & Arnetoli, G. (1998). Eye movement abnormalities in anorexia nervosa. *Psychiatry Research, 78,* 59-70.

Paul, T., Schroeter, K., Dahme, B., & Nutzinger, D. O. (2002). Self-injurious behavior in women with eating disorders. *Am J Psychiatry, 159,* 408-411.

Penas-Lledo, E., Vaz, F. J., Ramos, M. I., & Waller, G. (2002). Impulsive behaviours in bulimic patients: Relation to general psychopathology. *International Journal of Eating Disorders,* 32, 98-102.

Perpina, C., Hemsley, D., Treasure, J., & de Silva, P. (1993). Is the selective information processing of food and body words specific to patients with eating disorders? *International Journal of Eating Disorders.,* 14, 359-366.

Pieters, G., Sabbe, B., Hulstijn, W., Probst, M., Vandereyken, W., & Peuskens, J. (2003). Fast psychomotor functioning in underweight anorexia nervosa patients. *Journal of Psychiatric Research,* 37, 501-508.

Quraishi, S. & Frangou, S. (2002). Neuropsychology of bipolar disorder: A review. *Journal of Affective Disorders,* 72, 209-226.

Ranseen, J. D. & Humphries, L. L. (1992). The intellectual functioning of eating disorder patients. *Journal of the American Academy of Child & Adolescent Psychiatry,* 31, 844-846.

Rastam, M. (1992). Anorexia nervosa in 51 sweedish adolescents: Premorbid problems and comorbidity. *Academy of Child and Adolescent Psychiatry,* 31, 819-829.

Robbins, T. W. (1996). Dissociating executive functions of the prefrontal cortex. *Philosophical Transactions:Biological Sciences,* 351, 1463-1471.

Rubia, K. (2002). The dynamic approach to neurodevelopmental psychiatric disorders: Use of fMRI combined with neuropsychology to elucidate the dynamics of psychiatric disorders, exemplified in ADHD and schizophrenia. *Behavioural Brain Research,* 130, 47-56.

Seed, J. A., Dixon, R. A., McCluskey, S. E., & Young, A. H. (2000). Basal activity of the hypo-thalamic-pituitary-adrenal axis and cognitive function in anorexia nervosa. *Eur.Arch.Psychiatry Clin.Neurosci.,* 250, 11-15.

Seed, J. A., Mccue, P. M., Wesnes, K. A., Dahabra, S., & Young, A. H. (2002). Basal activity of the HPA axis and cognitive function in anorexia nervosa. *International Journal of Neuropsychopharmacology,* 5, 17-25.

Sein, P., Pearson, S., Nicol, A. R., & Hall, K. (1981). Anorexia nervosa and pseudoatrophy of the brain. *British Journal of Psychiatry,* 139, 257-258.

Shoebridge, P. & Gowers, S. G. (2000). Parental high concern and adolescent-onset anorexia nervosa. A case- control study to investigate direction of causality. *Br.J.Psychiatry,* 176, 132-137.

Sohlberg, S., Norring, C., Holmgren, S., & Rosmark, B. (1989). Impulsivity and the long term prognosis of psychiatric patients with anorexia nervosa or bulimia nervosa. *Journal of Nervous and Mental Disease,* 249-258.

Sohlberg, S. & Strober, M. (1994). Personality in Anorexia-Nervosa - An Update and A Theoretical Integration. *Acta Psychiatrica Scandinavica,* 89, 1-15.

Speranza, M., Corcos, M., Godart, N., Jeammet, P., & Flament, M. (2001). Current and lifetime prevalence of obsessive compulsive disorders in eating disorders. *Encephale-Revue de Psychiatrie Clinique Biologique et Therapeutique,* 27, 541-550.

Spinella, M. (2004). Neurobehavioral correlates of impulsivity: Evidence of prefrontal involvement. *International Journal of Neuroscience.,* 114, 95-104.

Spreen, O. & Strauss, E. (1998). Executive functions. In O.Spreen & E. Strauss (Eds.), *A Compendium of Neuropsychological Tests Administration, Norms and Commentry* (2nd ed., pp. 171-231). New York: Oxford University Press.

Srinivasagam, N. M., Kaye, W. H., Plotnicov, K. H., Greeno, C., Weltzin, T. E., & Rao, R. (1995). Persistent perfectionism, symmetry, and exactness after long-term recovery from anorexia nervosa. *American Journal of Psychiatry.,* 152, 1630-1634.

Steiger, H., Israel, M., Gauvin, L., Kin, N. M. K. N. Y., & Young, S. N. (2003). Implications of compulsive and impulsive traits for serotonin status in women with bulimia nervosa. *Psychiatry Research.,* 120, 219-229.

Strober, M. (2004). Pathologic fear conditioning and anorexia nervosa: On the search for novel paradigms. *International Journal of Eating Disorders,* 35, 504-508.

Strupp, B. J., Weingartner, H., Kaye, W., & Gwirtsman, H. (1986). Cognitive Processing in Anorexia-Nervosa: A Disturbance in Automatic Information-Processing. *Neuropsychobiology,* 15, 89-94.

Sutandar-Pinnock, K., Woodside, D. B., Carter, J. C., Olmsted, M. P., & Kaplan, A. S. (2003). Perfectionism in anorexia nervosa: A 6-24-month follow-up study. *International Journal of Eating Disorders,* 33, 225-229.

Swann, A. C., Bjork, J. M., Moeller, F. G., & Dougherty, D. M. (2002). Two models of impulsivity: Relationship to personality traits and psychopathology. *Biological Psychiatry,* 51, 988-994.

Szmukler, G. I., Andrewes, D., Kingston, K., & Chen, L. (1992). Neuropsychological impairment in anorexia nervosa: Before and after refeeding. *Journal of Clinical & Experimental Neuropsychology,* 14, 347-352.

Tchanturia, K., Campbell, I., Morris, R. G., & Treasure, J. (2005). Neuropsychological studies in anorexia nervosa. *International Journal of Eating Disorders, In Press.*

Tchanturia, K., Anderluh, M. B., Morris, R. G., Rabe-Hesketh, S., Collier, D. A., Sanchez, P. et al. (2004a). Cognitive flexibility in anorexia nervosa and bulimia nervosa. *Journal of the International Neuropsychological Society,* 10, 513-520.

Tchanturia, K., Morris, R. G., Brecelj Anderluh, M., Collier, D. A., Nikolaou, V., & Treasure, J. (2004b). Set shifting in anorexia nervosa: an examination before and after weight gain, in full recovery and relationship to childhood and adult OCPD traits. *Journal of Psychiatric Research,* 38, 545-552.

Tchanturia, K., Morris, R. G., Surguladze, S., & Treasure, J. (2002). An examination of perceptual and cognitive set shifting tasks in acute anorexic nervosa and following recovery. *Eating & Weight Disorders,* 7, 312-315.

Tchanturia, K., Serpell, L., Troop, N., & Treasure, J. (2001). Perceptual illusions in eating disorders: Rigid and fluctuating styles. *Journal of Behavior Therapy & Experimental Psychiatry.,* 107-115.

Tchanturia, K., Uher, R., Liao, T., Campbell, I., & Treasure, J. (2005). Decision making in eating disorders. *In progress*.

Toner, B. B., Garfinkel, P. E., & Garner, D. M. (1987). Cognitive style of patients with bulimic and diet-restricting anorexia nervosa. *American Journal of Psychiatry.,* 144, 510-512.

Touyz, S. W., Beumont, P. J. V., & Johnstone, L. C. (1986). Neuropsychological correlates of dieting disorders. *International Journal of Eating Disorders.,* 5, 1025-1034.

Uher, R., Brammer, M. J., Murphy, T., Campbell, I. C., Ng, V. W., Williams, S. C. R. et al. (2003). Recovery and chronicity in anorexia nervosa: Brain activity associated with differential outcomes. *Biological Psychiatry,* 54, 934-942.

Uher, R., Murphy, T., Brammer, M. J., Dalgleish, T., Phillips, M. L., Ng, V. W. et al. (2004). Medial prefrontal cortex activity associated with symptom provocation in eating disorders. *American Journal of Psychiatry,* 161, 1238-1246.

Uher, R., Treasure, J., & Campbell, I. C. (2002). Neuroanatomical bases of eating disorders. In H.D'haenen, J.A.den Boer, & P.Willner (Eds.), *Textbook of Biological Psychiatry* (pp. 1173-1180). Chichester: John Wiley & Sons.

Vedhara, K., Hyde, J., Gilchrist, I. D., Tytherleigh, M., & Plummer, S. (2000). Acute stress, memory, attention and cortisol. *Psychoneuroendocrinology,* 25, 535-549.

Vitousek, K. & Manke, F. (1994). Personality variables and disorders in anorexia nervosa and bulimia nervosa. *J Abnorm.Psychol,* 103, 137-147.

von Ranson, K. M., Kaye, W. H., Weltzin, T. E., Rao, R., & Matsunaga, H. (1999). Obsessive-compulsive disorder symptoms before and after recovery from bulimia nervosa. *American Journal of Psychiatry, 156,* 1703-1708.

Witt, E. D., Ryan, C., & Hsu, L. G. (1985). Learning deficits in adolescents with anorexia nervosa. *Journal of Nervous & Mental Disease, 173,* 182-184.

INDEX

A

B

C

D

E

F

G

H

I

K

L

M

N

O